Tom Slemen
MYSTERIES

© Tom Slemen 2002

Published by The Bluecoat Press, Liverpool
Book design by March Design, Liverpool
Printed by Universities Press, Belfast

ISBN 1 872568 98 X

Tom Slemen
MYSTERIES

The Bluecoat Press

CONTENTS

INTRODUCTION

The mysteries which are catalogued on the following pages are not concerned with inanimate riddles such as the Bermuda Triangle, or the UFO phenomenon, but with conundrums centred on people. Again and again while researching this book, I unearthed information on mysterious people which was maddeningly scanty. One such example concerns Jechiele, a French rabbi who had an electric light – in the thirteenth century!

The contemporary chroniclers merely give us a tantalising glimpse of this strange individual by telling us that Jechiele discouraged unwanted visitors from knocking on his door by discharging a 'fiery blue spark' from a curious apparatus in his study to the door-knocker via a wire. Callers who were unfortunate enough to be holding the knocker when the blue spark was crackling, would be flung back from the doorstep by the invisible power. Each night Jechiele could be seen through the window in his study, working by the light of 'a peculiar blue lamp that had neither oil nor wick'. What is more, this lamp somehow managed to light itself. What was Jechiele working on in his study? Frustratingly, the chroniclers never answered that question.

Jechiele is just one of many mysterious geniuses who have been omitted from the history books, and there are striking omissions as far as ordinary people are concerned too. Take the case of the first woman in space – the history books record that Russian cosmonaut, Valentina Tereshkova, was the first female to orbit the earth (48 times) in June 1963, but two years before, on 17 February 1961, tracking stations around the world picked up the launch of a manned space probe from the USSR, and one of the cosmonauts who was heard chatting to her colleagues in the craft was a woman who did not identify herself. The Russians didn't even announce the launch of the craft, which orbited the earth in an erratic trajectory. The following enigmatic comment was made by the unnamed female cosmonaut: "It's difficult … [static] … if we don't get out, the world will never hear about it …"

Seven days later, the radio telescopes at the tracking stations of Uppsala, Bochum, Turin and Meudon picked up the final horrifying transmission from the ill-starred cosmonauts. The tapes of the distressing dialogue have never been released. Space experts and military scientists who analysed the bizarre trajectory of the doomed spaceship conjectured that the craft had made an unsuccessful attempt to orbit the Moon, but had lacked sufficient speed to break away from the Earth's gravitational pull. Whatever the cause of the tragedy, the unknown Russian space pioneers remain anonymous, even in death.

A more recent example of a less illustrious but equally mysterious person, on whom we have scarcely any data, is the 'M4 Girl' – a young woman who was found wandering in a confused state along the hard shoulder of the M4 motorway near the Severn Bridge in November 1988. She failed to respond to questioning by the police and several doctors. The silent woman was taken to a Bristol Hospital and a description of her was circulated to police forces throughout Britain.

Shortly afterwards, a man and a woman from Crediton, near Exeter, in Devon, came forward claiming that they were the girl's parents. They took her home with them, but it was never revealed who she was, or why she was walking alone along a motorway, 80 miles from home. The couple from Devon requested anonymity and, for some inexplicable reason, a phalanx of hard-boiled journalists who had been keenly following the case, quickly dropped the story. The autistic-like girl later became something of a cult figure when the pop group Marillion released their concept album, Brave, which was inspired by the incident.

Another mysterious individual who has provided us with insufficient data to satisfy our curiosity, is the young man in a white T-shirt who apparently walked through a solid door in a Lancashire nightclub. If this strange feat had not been captured on a security video camera, it would certainly have been dismissed as an incredible yarn, but the video tape has been analysed by BBC television technicians, and they have declared it to be genuine.

This eerie incident unfolded in the early hours of 27 October 1991, at the Butterflies nightclub in Oldham. The digital clock on the security video camera read 4.32am and the club was deserted, when the burglar alarm suddenly went off. At that precise moment, the 'thing' that had triggered the alarm was captured on a security video camera: it was a semi-transparent young man in a white T-shirt passing through a solid locked door. The brief footage shows him prowling the corridors of the empty club like a thief in the night. But this was no ordinary prowler, for when the police and the club's manager and assistant manager arrived at the locked-up premises, there were no physical signs of a break-in, and there was no trace of the spectral burglar.

When the police viewed the tape of the translucent intruder, they were amazed by the sight of the figure passing through the closed door. The tape was taken to the BBC and handed over to a group of technicians who employed a simple test to discover whether the tape was a hoax. Using the latest micro-chip technology, they found that there was only one video signal on the tape – and this meant that no one had tampered with it. So the tape was genuine – but who was the intruder? No one knows. It was naturally assumed at the time that he was a ghost, but the nightclub has no history of hauntings. The anonymous prowler, consigned to the supernatural dustbin, is yet another example of those shadowy individuals featured in this book: the mysterious people.

THE COUNT OF ST GERMAIN
The Real Doctor Who?

When the English soldiers returned from the Holy Land after the third Crusade came to a disastrous end in the 12th century, they brought back with them many fabulous tales of the mysterious Orient.

One particular story which they often told was of a man known in the East as the 'Wandering Jew'. The story went as follows:

In the Judgement Hall of Pontius Pilate, there was a Jewish doorkeeper named Cartaphilus, who had actually been present at the trial of Jesus of Nazareth. When Christ was dragging his cross through the streets on the way to Calvary, he halted for a moment to rest, and at this point, Cartaphilus stepped out from the large crowd lining the route and told Jesus to hurry up. Jesus looked at Cartaphilus. "I will go now, but thou shall wait until I return," he said.

The Roman soldiers escorting Christ to the crucifixion site roughly pushed Cartaphilus back into the crowd, and Jesus slowly continued on his way. Cartaphilus had no idea what Jesus had meant until, many years later, he realised that all his friends were gradually dying of old age, while he had not aged at all. Each day the doorkeeper would remember Christ's words and shudder. He eventually realised that he was condemned to wander the earth, without ageing, until Christ's Second Coming.

This tale was dismissed by the religious authorities of the day as an apocryphal yarn, and the legend of the Wandering Jew was later interpreted by the Christians as an allegorical story, symbolising the global wanderings and persecutions of the Jewish race because of their refusal to accept Jesus as the long-awaited Messiah.

The tale gradually passed into European folklore and joined the other myths of the Middle Ages. Then, in the 13th century, a number of travellers returning to England from the Continent spoke of meeting, or hearing of, a strange blasphemous man who claimed he had been around when Christ was on earth. These curious reports were later strengthened in 1228 when an Armenian Archbishop visited St Albans. He told his astonished audience that he had recently dined with an unusual man who confessed to being Cartaphilus, the man who had mocked Christ.

Many more encounters with Cartaphilus were reported in the following centuries, and each meeting seemed to occur nearer and nearer to Western Europe.

Then one day in 1740, a mysterious man dressed in black arrived in Paris. The gaudily-dressed, fashion-conscious Parisians instantly noticed the sinister stranger, and admired the dazzling collection of diamond rings on each of his fingers. The man in black also wore diamond-encrusted shoe-buckles, a display of wealth which suggested that he was an aristocrat, although nobody in Paris could identify him. From the Jewish cast of his handsome countenance, some of the superstitious citizens of Paris believed him to be Cartaphilus, the Wandering Jew. The man of mystery later identified himself as the Count of St Germain, and he was quickly welcomed by the nobility into the fashionable circles of Parisian life.

In the distinguished company of writers, philosophers, scientists, freemasons and aristocrats, the Count displayed a veritable plethora of talents. He was an accomplished pianist, a gifted singer and violinist, a linguist who spoke fluent Spanish, Greek, Italian, Russian, Portuguese, Chinese, Arabic, Sanskrit, English and, of course, French. The Count of St Germain was also a fine artist, an historian, and a brilliant alchemist. He maintained that he had travelled widely, and recounted his many visits to the court of the Shah of Persia, where he had learned the closely-guarded science of improving and enlarging gemstones. The Count also hinted that he had learned many arcane lessons of the occult.

But what stunned his awestruck listeners most was his seemingly preposterous claim that he was over a thousand years old. This assertion came about one evening when the conversation turned to religious matters. The Count movingly described Christ as if he had personally known him, and talked in detail of the miraculous water-into-wine event at the marriage feast of Cana as if he were describing a party-trick. After this peculiar anecdote, the Count became tearful, and in a broken, uncharacteristically sombre voice, declared that he had always known that Christ would meet a bad end.

The Count of St Germain also spoke of other historical celebrities as if he had been an eyewitness to their deeds. Whenever sceptical historians tried to trip up the Count by questioning him about trivial historical details that were not widely known, the Count would always reply with astonishing accuracy, leaving the questioner thoroughly perplexed.

The Count's claim to be much older than he looked was reinforced one day when the aged Countess von Georgy was introduced to him. She immediately recognised the enigmatic nobleman as the same individual she had met 50 years previously in Venice, where she had been the ambassadress. But she was amazed that the Count still looked the same age as he had then, which was about 45. The Countess was naturally confused by this, and asked him if his father had been in Venice at that time. The Count shook his head and told her that it had been he, and proceeded to baffle the Countess by telling her how beautiful she had looked as a young woman and how he had enjoyed playing her favourite musical piece on the violin. The Countess recoiled in disbelief and cried, "Why, you must be almost one hundred years old."

"That is not impossible," replied the Count, enigmatically.

"You are a most extraordinary man!" exclaimed the old Countess. "A devil!"

The comparison to a demon touched a sore point in the Count, and in a raised voice, he replied, "For pity's sake! No such names!" He then turned his back on the shocked Countess and stormed out of the room.

The king of France, Louis XV, was intrigued by the stories of the mysterious Count St Germain. He sought him out and offered him an invitation to attend the royal court. The Count accepted the invitation, and succeeded in captivating the king and his courtiers, as well as Madame de Pompadour, the king's mistress. During the spectacular banquets that were regularly held at the court, the Count would abstain from food and wine, but would sometimes sip mineral water instead. Furthermore, when the Count did dine, it was always in private. Precisely what he consumed is not known, although some of the courtiers claimed he was a vegetarian.

In 1745, the year of the Jacobite Rebellion in Britain, Count St Germain turned up in London, where he was arrested on a charge of spying. Horace Walpole, the son of Sir Robert Walpole, Britain's first Prime Minister, mentioned the incident in a letter to his lifelong correspondent, Sir Horace Mann. Walpole wrote:

The other day they seized an odd man who goes by the name of the Count St Germain. He has been here these two years, and will not tell who he is, or whence he came, but professes that he does not go by his right name. He sings and plays on the violin wonderfully, is mad and not very sensible.

At a time when English xenophobia was at an all-time high, because many foreigners, especially Frenchmen, were known to be sympathetic to the Jacobite cause, the Count should have been imprisoned. But instead, he was allowed his freedom. Just why this was, is still a mystery. One curious report which circulated at the time claimed that the Count used hypnotic suggestion to 'persuade' his detainers that he was innocent. This is a real possibility: Anton Mesmer, who is credited with the discovery of hypnotism, had stated years before that the Count possessed a 'vast understanding of the workings of the human mind' and had been directly responsible for teaching him the art of hypnosis.

In 1756, the Count was spotted by Sir Robert Clive in India, and in 1760, history records that King Louis XV sent Monsieur St Germain to The Hague to help settle the peace treaty between Prussia and Austria. In 1762, the Count took part in the deposition of Peter III of Russia and also played an active role in bringing Catherine the Great to the throne.

The Count St Germain opened a mass-production factory in Venice in 1769, where he developed a synthetic form of silk. During this period he also executed several magnificent sculptures in the tradition of the classical Greeks. A year later he was again actively involved in the politics of other nations; this time he was seen in the uniform of a Russian General with Prince Alexei Orloff in Leghorn!

After the death of Louis XV in 1774, the man from nowhere turned up unexpectedly again in Paris and warned the new monarch, King Louis XVI and his Queen, Marie Antoinette, of the approaching danger of the French Revolution, which he described as a 'gigantic conspiracy' that would overthrow the order of things. Of course, the warning went unheeded, and among the final entries in her diary, Marie Antoinette recorded her regret at not taking the Count's advice.

In February 1784, Prince Charles of Hesse-Cassel, Germany, announced the news that the Count was dead, and was to be buried at the local church in Eckenforde. Among the crowds that attended the funeral service were many prominent occultists, including Count Cagliostro, Anton Mesmer, and the philosopher, Louis St Martin. The coffin was lowered into the grave, and many of the mourners sobbed at what seemed so unbelievable: the death of the immortal Count. But that is not the end of the story ...

A year later, a congress of Freemasons was held in Paris. Among the Rosicrucians, Kabbalists and Illuminati was the supposedly dead Count St Germain. Thirty-six years after his funeral, the Count was seen by scores of people in Paris. These included the diarist Mademoiselle d'Adhemar, and the educationalist Madame de Genlis. Both women said the Count still looked like a 45-year-old.

In 1870 the Emperor Napoleon III was so fascinated by the reports of 'The Undying Count' that he ordered a special commission to be set up at the Hotel de Ville to investigate the nobleman. But the findings of the commission never came to a conclusion because, in 1871, a mysterious fire gutted the Hotel de Ville, destroying every document that related to the self-styled Count.

The Count of St Germain was then briefly seen in Milan in 1867, attending a meeting of the Grand Lodge of Freemasons. In 1896, the theosophist Annie Besant said she had met the Count, and around the same year, Russian theosophist Madame Blavatsky claimed the Count had been in contact with her. She even went so far as to proclaim that he belonged to a race of immortals who lived in a subterranean country called Shambhala, north of the Himalayas.

In 1897, the French singer Emma Calve also claimed that the Count had paid her a visit, and she called him a 'great chiromancer' who had told her many truths.

The story of the immortal Count went out of vogue at the beginning of the 20th century – until August 1914, in the early days of World War One, when two Bavarian soldiers captured a Jewish-looking Frenchman in Alsace. As a prisoner of war he was subjected to an all-night interrogation, during which he stubbornly refused to reveal his name. Suddenly, in the early hours of the morning, the unidentified Frenchman became very irritable and started to rant about the futility of the war. He told his captors, "Throw down your guns! The war will end in 1918 with defeat for the German nation and her allies!"

One of the soldiers, Andreas Rill, laughed at the prisoner's words. He thought that the man was merely expressing the hopes of every Frenchman, but he was nevertheless intrigued by the prisoner's other prophecies.

"Everyone will be a millionaire after the war!" he predicted. "There will be so much money in circulation that people will throw it from windows and no one will bother to pick it up. You will need to carry it around in wheelbarrows to buy a loaf of bread!"

Was he referring to the rampant inflation of post-World War One Germany?

The soldiers scoffed at the predictions, but they allowed the prophet to ramble on. He gave them more future 'history' lessons:

"After the confetti money will come the anti-Christ – a tyrant from the lower classes who will wear an ancient symbol. He will lead Germany into another global war in 1939, but will be defeated six years on after doing inhuman, unspeakable things."

At this point the Frenchman started to become incoherent. He started to sing, then began to sob. Thinking he was mad, the soldiers took pity on him and decided to let him go, and he disappeared back into obscurity. His identity is still unknown. Could he have been the mysterious Count of St Germain?

Today, most historians regard the Count of St Germain as nothing more than a silver-tongued charlatan. But there are so many unanswered questions. What was the source of the Count's wealth? How can we possibly explain his longevity? For that matter, where did he come from? If he had been an impostor, surely someone would have recognised him?

The only surviving manuscript written by the Count, entitled *La Trés Sainte Trinosophie* is in the library at Troyes, France, and to date, it has resisted every attempt to be fully deciphered, but one decoded section of the text states:

We moved through space at a speed that can be compared with nothing itself. Within a fraction of a second the plains below us were out of sight and the Earth had become a faint nebula.

What does this signify? Could it be that the Count of St Germain was some type of traveller in space and time? A renegade timelord from the future who liked to meddle with history? If this were so, perhaps he really had talked with Christ and the kings of bygone days.

WILLIAM HARRISON
The Bizarre Case of the Campden 'Murder'

On 16 August 1660, 70-year-old William Harrison, conscientious steward to Lady Campden, set out on a three-mile walk from the English town of Chipping Campden to Charringworth in the Cotswold hills. He was off to collect rent for Lady Campden, and had told his wife that he expected to be home by early evening at the latest.

By 8pm Harrison's wife was still waiting for him to return. She had a strange feeling that something had happened to her husband, so she sent out a servant named John Perry to look for him. The hours dragged by, but there was still no news of Harrison – or Perry. By 3am, Mrs Harrison was frantic with worry and sent her son Edward out to look for the missing men. Edward met John Perry on the road leading to Charringworth, and the servant said he had looked everywhere for Mr Harrison but that he was nowhere to be seen. Edward and Perry embarked on another search of the surrounding countryside, but failed to find any trace of the missing man.

On their way back from the futile search, they met a man who told them that William Harrison's hat and collar had been found covered in blood by the roadside. Both articles had been slashed with a blade. News of the suspected murder swept through the town of Chipping Campden, and a massive search party headed out of the town and into the countryside. The woods were thoroughly searched, and every ditch was painstakingly inspected, but no vestiges of Harrison, nor any evidence of foul play were found. The traumatised Mrs Harrison started yelling at John Perry, accusing him of being a murderer and a robber.

Perry was brought before the magistrate on the following morning and interrogated about his movements on the day of the disappearance. Perry confessed that he had not searched for Mr Harrison as Mrs Harrison had instructed, because he was scared to go into the countryside on his own in the dark, but he had been too ashamed to return to the village to admit this. He had spent the night cowering in a hen-roost until midnight, when a full moon came out from behind the clouds to light up the countryside. Perry claimed that he had then mustered up enough courage to begin the search, but became lost when a thick mist developed. He had ended up sleeping under a hedge.

The magistrate was angered by the unbelievable yarn, and Perry was kept in custody for a week while another search was made for Harrison. But this hunt was also in vain. It was as if William Harrison had vanished into thin air.

That week, Perry suddenly announced that he had information relating to the mysterious disappearance of his master, but was only prepared to communicate his knowledge to the magistrate. His wish was granted, and Perry told the magistrate that he knew for sure that Harrison had been murdered, but could not reveal the name of the killer for personal reasons. The magistrate demanded to know the murderer's identity and grilled the servant for hours, until finally, Perry broke down and confessed that his own mother and brother had killed the missing man.

The magistrate was furious. He had known the servant's mother for years, and refused to believe John Perry's accusation. But the servant was adamant that he was telling the truth, and started to elaborate on the causes of the murder.

"Ever since I took up my post at the Harrison household, my family have been urging me to steal little things for them," he said. "They recently started to become interested in when the rent was being collected by Mr Harrison, so that they could waylay him. I told them I would not become involved with such a crime, but my mother kept reminding me how poor the family was. They pressured me so hard that eventually I told them what they wanted to know – what routes Harrison took at certain times, and the amount he would be carrying. They planned to knock him unconscious before making off with the rent money, but the old man cried out for help, and my brother panicked and strangled him. He and my mother dumped the body in a field before making off with the money."

"Then how did they forget to hide the hat and collar that were found?" demanded the magistrate.

Perry told him that his mother and brother had deliberately left the items at the roadside to mislead any searchers. Joan Perry and her son Richard were arrested, and although no body was found at the spot in the field specified by the servant, Joan and Richard had no alibi for the time of the murder.

In September, Joan, Richard – and John Perry, were brought before Sir Christopher Turnor at Gloucester Assizes. The judge said that as there was no body, there was no evidence that a murder had been committed. But as Joan and Richard sighed with relief at the judge's ruling, another case was introduced against them – a separate case – of robbery. A year earlier, William Harrison's house had been broken into and the thieves – who were never caught – made off with a sum of £140. In the light of the murder accusation, the Perrys seemed to be the only natural suspects.

They were advised to confess to the robbery without fear of any punishment, because of the Act of Pardon and Oblivion issued by King Charles II. This unusual act was introduced to forgive the horrors perpetrated during the Civil Wars, and it covered any crimes prior to May 1660. So, with the act in mind, the Perrys decided to confess to the robbery, knowing that they would be pardoned. They duly were, but the judge then placed the murder case before Sir Robert Hyde. In March 1661, Hyde sentenced John Perry and his mother and brother to death. It had been a peculiar case. John Perry had changed his testimony, instead claiming that he had been in a state of insanity when he made his original statement. He swore that he had made up the story about the killing of Harrison, but the court assumed that the servant was simply trying to talk his way out of being hanged.

So it was, that on Broadway Hill, the Perrys were hanged one after the other. Until the moment when the noose broke their necks, they screamed out their innocence. Not one of the jeering spectators was prepared to believe their desperate claims. So imagine how these people felt when William Harrison turned up in good health a year after the executions.

Harrison strolled into Chipping Campden two years after his supposed murder and informed his nonplussed wife that he had spent the last couple of years working as a slave in Turkey! He related how, on the day of his disappearance, he had been attacked by three men who took him on horseback across England to Deal in Kent, where he was put on board a ship. The ship sailed off, but weeks into the voyage, it was captured by Turkish pirates, who took all the passengers to a slave market in Turkey. Old Harrison was purchased by a wealthy 80-year-old Turkish doctor, who employed the Englishman as a servant in his house. After a year in the service of the doctor, Harrison noticed that his master's health was worsening. When the doctor suddenly dropped dead, Harrison seized his chance and sold his deceased master's belongings and made enough money to pay for his passage home.

Nobody in the town believed this incredible, far-fetched tale, but Harrison stuck by his story for the rest of his days.

Could it be that Harrison really spent his two missing years trying to start a new life somewhere in England – perhaps with a mistress? If something of this nature was the case, it would have been totally out of character for a man who had faithfully served Lady Campden and appeared to cherish his wife. But surely his exotic adventure was purely a romantic invention – unless, as the old saying goes, stranger things happen at sea.

HARRY AGANNIS
The Dead Man Who Helped Telly Savalas

Shortly after 3am on the morning of 27 February 1957, the late American actor Telly Savalas – famous for his role as Theo Kojak in the television series of the 1970s – was driving home from his cousin's house on Long Island, New York. Halfway through the homeward journey, Savalas heard the engine of his car splutter, before stalling, and he realised he'd run out of gas. The actor left the car and walked through heavy rain to the red neon-sign burning in the distance. It turned out to be an all-night diner. A young man at the counter told Savalas how to get to the nearest garage. He walked outside and pointed to a poorly-lit lane, and said, "Walk right down there, sir, and you will come to a freeway. Turn right at the freeway and you will see a gas station about three hundred yards away." Savalas thanked the man and set off down the dark secluded lane.

He was halfway down the lane when he heard a noise behind him. Savalas turned, and saw a black Cadillac crawling along the road with its headlights off. The driver wound his side window down and shouted in a high-pitched voice, "Do you want a lift?" Savalas was obviously wary about accepting lifts from strangers in the dead of night in New York – especially from drivers snaking about with no lights – but there was something trustworthy about the driver. He seemed quite sane and decent, and the rain was heavy, so Savalas decided to accept the stranger's kind offer. He got in the vehicle and sat in the front passenger seat.

"Where do you want to go?" asked the driver.

"Er, the nearest gas station, please. You turn right at the end of this lane and it's three hundred yards down the freeway," Savalas replied.

The man didn't speak, and there was an eeriness about him that unnerved Savalas. No attempt at conversation was made. The driver just sat and looked over the wheel and didn't seem to blink. He stared at the lane ahead with a grave look.

"Where are you headed yourself?" the actor asked, struggling to keep the concern out of his voice. He surveyed the man's smart attire: a black tuxedo, white silk shirt and a black bow tie. His raven hair was oiled and slicked back, and he had a little, well-trimmed toothbrush mustache.

"To the crossroads to meet my destiny," came the lugubrious reply.

Savalas just said, "Oh," and assumed the man was either drunk, or mad. He was rapidly beginning to regret taking the lift from the stranger, but the journey continued without any more dialogue. Even so, Savalas was only too eager to leave the uncommunicative driver when the gas station finally loomed through the rain-lashed windshield. But before he left the car, Savalas felt compelled to offer the man a couple of dollars for giving him the lift. It was then that Savalas realised, to his embarrassment, that he had left his wallet at his cousin's house. Still, he was keen to pay the man at a later time, so he asked the driver for his name and address. The man was very reluctant and strangely nervous about giving the details, but at last he told the actor that his name was Harry Agannis, and he gave a South Manhattan address and a phone number which Savalas scribbled down on a piece of notepaper. He also offered a dollar bill to Savalas, and told him, "Please take it for your gas. Go on."

Savalas took the money and thanked Agannis, then ran through the downpour to the gas station. When he reached the station, he turned to wave to Agannis – but the Cadillac had gone.

Rather appropriately, Savalas had just landed a starring role in an episode of Rod Serling's *The Twilight Zone* when, a couple of days later, he found the note with Agannis's address and phone number in the inside pocket of his jacket. He decided to telephone him to say he'd be over soon to pay him. Savalas got an engaged tone the first time, so he tried again, and a woman answered, "Joan Agannis. Hello?"

"Could I speak to Harry Agannis please?" Savalas asked politely.

There was a silent pause, then in a broken voice the woman said, "What? Is this some kind of sick joke? Who are you?"

Savalas was baffled, but he managed to calm the woman down and told her he was serious, upon which she burst into tears. Savalas, was not ready for her reaction and found it irritating.

"Look, have I dialled the right number, for cryin' out loud? What's up?"

"My husband ..." began Mrs Agannis, her sobs slowly subsiding. "My husband died three years ago."

"That's impossible," Savalas said, and he repeated the name of the man he'd written on the note.

"That's right. Harry Agannis. He's dead. What do you want?"

Without giving Savalas the chance to reply, she slammed down the phone.

He was completely intrigued – and a little scared – but he decided to drive to the woman's house. When Mrs Agannis answered the door, he explained who he was and showed her his Actor's Union card. She awkwardly admitted him into her home. She showed Savalas the photograph of her deceased husband. Without doubt it was the same man who had given him a lift. Same toothbrush mustache and dark, slicked-back hairstyle. The actor shuddered when he saw the photograph. She explained to him that in February 1954 her husband had been returning from a high-school reunion party around 3am – dressed in a tuxedo, exactly as Savalas had described – when the Cadillac he was driving was involved in an horrific crash at the crossroads, half a mile from the gas station where the actor had been dropped off. The Cadillac had skidded into a truck and burst into flames. The truck driver survived, and even tried to free Mr Agannis from the burning wreckage of his car, but his legs were trapped. The trucker managed to retrieve a fire extinguisher from his crashed vehicle, and tried to use it to douse the flames from the burning Cadillac – but the extinguisher was faulty, and failed to work. Harry Agannis screamed as the flames rose around him, slowly engulfing both him and the car. In a state of shocked helplessness, the trucker punched Agannis repeatedly in the face until he was unconscious, in order to put an end to his suffering and stifle his agonising screams. Seconds later, the Cadillac erupted into a huge fireball which burned the trucker's face and arms.

Up until his death in 1994, Telly Savalas was haunted by the memory of that awful rainy night, and he refused to travel anywhere near the area of Long Island, where he believed a dead man had given him a lift.

Thomas Blood
Cunning Criminal or Wily Double Agent?

1671 was a year of unlimited opportunity for two of history's greatest adventurers. In the West Indies that year, the Welsh buccaneer Sir Henry Morgan was made Deputy Governor of Jamaica, while in England, self-styled 'Colonel' Thomas Blood was putting a plan into action that would result in the most daring robbery of all time: the theft of the Crown Jewels from the Tower of London.

Thomas Blood (alias Ayliffe, aka Allen) was born in 1618, the son of an Irish blacksmith. Information on his early life is very scant, but it is known that he served the Parliamentary cause during the English Civil War. Just exactly what Blood's role was during the war isn't known, but he seems to have been involved in espionage, and he was rewarded for his services with considerable estates in Ireland. However, when the monarchy was restored in 1660, Blood lost his lands and his position, and became an embittered terrorist with a dark genius for ruthless schemes designed to disrupt and intimidate his aristocratic enemies. But long before he fell on hard times. Blood was a mysterious individual who expressed no particular allegiance to any religion or political wing, unless it suited his own ends. It is easy to dismiss him as an adventurer, but Blood's behaviour suggests that he may have been in the pay of someone. Behind all of his 'who dares wins' exploits, there are tantalising glimpses of a man who was somebody's agent. Many suspected him of being a spy – but a spy for whom?

In 1633, Blood and a group of abettors tried to kidnap the Duke of Ormonde, the Lord Lieutenant of Ireland, at Dublin Castle, but the conspirators were betrayed, and all but Blood were captured and thrown into prison. A reward was offered for Blood's capture – dead or alive – but he apparently wasn't too worried about the price on his head, for he attempted – unsuccessfully – to free his co-conspirators, and was forced to flee to Holland.

In 1639, Blood was active among the Fifth Monarchy Men, an extreme Puritan sect who literally believed that the 'fifth monarchy', foretold in the *Book of Daniel*, was at hand. The biblical prophecy claimed that a fifth monarchy of Christ would succeed the rule of the Assyrians, the Persians, the Greeks and the Romans. The sect was led by Thomas Venner, a religious fanatic, who launched two abortive risings in 1657 and 1661. Venner was subsequently captured and executed but Blood got away Scot-free. In fact, the Irishman had an uncanny habit of leaving rebellious groups just as they were about to be eradicated. It was the same story when he joined the Covenanters – a group of Scottish Presbyterians who opposed the introduction of Charles I's religious policies into Scotland. Blood was right behind the movement and sat at the table with the counsel, but just days before the going got tough, and a confrontation with the king's troops was imminent, Blood was suddenly nowhere to be seen.

In 1667, Blood heard that an old militant acquaintance, a Captain Mason, was being taken under guard to a prison in York. With three accomplices, Blood rode up to the soldiers and opened fire on them. Captain Mason was rescued, and a badly-wounded Blood led him to safety. The price put on Blood's head was trebled, but the Irishman still managed to evade capture.

In 1670, Blood turned up in central London, where he perpetrated another audacious crime. He rode up to the coach carrying the Duke of Ormonde and yanked open the door. The terrified Duke was pulled from the coach by Blood and an accomplice and thrown onto the horse of another henchman, who rode as far as Tyburn before the cry went up that the nobleman had been kidnapped. The Duke was soon rescued, but Blood and his men escaped without harm.

This brings us to the event in 1671 for which Blood is best remembered: the theft of the Crown Jewels.

For several weeks, Thomas Blood, disguised as a parson, had been getting regularly acquainted with Talbot Edwards, the 77-year-old keeper of the Crown Jewels, in order to win his confidence. After just a few visits, the old man considered the 'parson' thoroughly trustworthy and completely above suspicion.

On 9 May at seven in the morning, Blood turned up in his clergyman guise for the last time with three accomplices. The keeper's daughter was around, so to keep her attention diverted, Blood introduced her to his 'nephew' – who was in fact the youngest accomplice, a fairly handsome man of about 25. As the couple began to chat, Blood steered the small-talk to the subject of the Jewels, and the keeper excitedly told Blood and his accomplices to follow him to the chamber of Martin Tower, where the Jewels were kept. Upon reaching the chamber, the old man turned to lock the door behind himself and the visitors, at which point Blood suddenly pulled a cloak over his head. The keeper struggled, and a gag was rammed into his mouth. Still the old man protested, so one of the thieves battered his head with a mallet before callously plunging a dagger into his stomach.

Blood then grabbed the mallet and used it to flatten St Edward's Crown so he could stuff it inside his coat. Another thief filed the sceptre in two, while the robber who had murdered the keeper stuffed the orb down his trousers as he laughed at his own exploits.

Then the unexpected happened. The son of the dead keeper turned up, and bumped into Blood's 'nephew', who was acting suspiciously, like a lookout. The son attacked him, but was coshed and gagged for his troubles.

The lookout then raced to the chamber and warned the others. Blood and his men instantly made a dash for it out of the chamber, and in the ensuing panic, the sceptre was dropped and left behind.

The son of the murdered keeper then regained consciousness, ripped the gag from his mouth, and raised the alarm, shouting, "Treason! Murder! The crown is stolen!"

Within seconds, the keeper's daughter arrived and clung to her brother in fear. One of the yeoman warders also answered the alert and challenged Blood squarely. The Colonel levelled his flintlock at him and blasted a hole in his chest, killing him instantly. As the fleeing gang headed for the Tower Wharf, they encountered another guard, but when he saw Blood and his men approaching, the yeoman got cold feet, dropped his musket and stepped aside, letting the thieves pass unchallenged.

The Tower was soon swarming with soldiers, and Blood's three accomplices were quickly captured. The Colonel's escape route was blocked by Captain Beckman, a fearless Civil War veteran, and the only man who managed to subdue the Irish daredevil. Blood was escorted to a cell in the Tower and interrogated for hours. But the prisoner insisted that he would talk to no one but the king about his deeds.

Two days later Blood's request was granted, and the miscreant was taken to Whitehall, where he had a lengthy conversation with King Charles II. Blood was taken back to the Tower, but was later inexplicably released and given a Royal pardon – as well as a 'pension' of £500. What is more, Blood's confiscated estates in Ireland were also restored to him.

Not long after all this, the English author and diarist John Evelyn was invited to dine at the king's table. When he arrived at the dinner, he was astounded to see Thomas Blood seated near the king. This did not make sense to Evelyn, who knew that the Irishman had served as a Parliamentarian in the Civil War and had made numerous kidnap attempts on the nobility. Yet, despite these crimes of treason, the attempted theft of the Crown Jewels and the murder of the old keeper who looked after them, Blood was apparently still held in favour by the king. And therein lies the mystery that has baffled generations of historians.

BRUCE LEE
Was the Martial Arts Superstar Murdered?

Bruce Lee was born in San Francisco on 27 November 1940, but was raised in Hong Kong, where he embarked on a movie career at the age of six. During his early teens, Bruce started to develop an interest in the martial arts. To harden his fists, he would pound them on a stool every day for hours, gradually transforming his hands into lethal, granite-hard weapons.

He returned to the United States when he was 18 in order to retain his American citizenship and enrolled as a Philosophy student at Washington University. Throughout his studies, Lee taught jeet-kune do (a hybrid discipline of kung fu and western pugilism) to provide him with an income of a few hundred dollars per week. One of his students, Linda Emery, was fascinated by her tutor, and she married him in 1964.

Lee then decided to quit his studies to rekindle his acting career in Hollywood and landed a role as Kato in *The Green Hornet* television series. He also gave martial arts lessons to some of the biggest movie stars in Los Angeles. For $150 an hour he taught some of his skills to James Coburn, Lee Marvin, James Garner and Steve McQueen.

Around this time, Warner Brothers were ready to produce *Kung Fu*, a groundbreaking television series about Kwai Chang Caine, a Buddhist monk trained in karate, who flees mainland China for the West after murdering a nobleman. Lee applied for the part of Caine, but Warner thought he was too inexperienced to play the role, which went to actor-dancer David Carradine instead. *Kung Fu* proved to be a success story in the United States and Europe, and is now regarded as a television cult classic.

Lee felt he had been denied stardom in the land of opportunity, so he returned to Hong Kong, where he struck up a partnership with Raymond Chow, an innovative film producer. The two men became the new wave of the Hong Kong film industry, and collaborated on some of the early kung fu blockbusters.

In 1971 Lee starred in his first Chinese action film, *The Big Boss*. He played the part of a new boy in an ice factory who helps striking workers with his breathtaking martial arts talent. The original cut was deemed to be too violent, the censors holding the film release date back for a year, and there was more trouble getting the film distributed, yet Lee continued to strive for international superstardom. He wrote, produced and directed *The Way of the Dragon* (1973), in which he cast himself as Tan Lung, an out-of-town strong arm who is paid by a Chinese restaurant owner in Rome to sort out the local Mafia menace.

Warner Brothers learned that the films were being received well, and were soon beating a path to Lee's door. They offered major financial support for Lee's next film, *Enter the Dragon* (1973). The film proved to be the success that had eluded Lee for so long, but tragically, the rising film star never got to enjoy the benefits of his achievement. While dubbing the film in Hong Kong on 10 May 1973, Bruce Lee collapsed. He recovered, but experienced respiratory problems, finding it difficult and exhausting to breathe. Even more seriously, he also suffered a series of convulsions which were put down to a swelling of his brain.

Lee was given Mannitol, an osmotic diuretic drug, which seemed to do the trick, and a week later, he appeared to be as fit as ever. In Los Angeles, Dr David Reisbord examined Lee. After a brain scan, a brain-flow study, a physical check-up, and an EEG analysis, Dr Reisbord told Lee that he had probably suffered a grand mal seizure – an indication of epilepsy, yet there were no indications as to why this was so. The brain scan showed no abnormalities, and other tests confirmed that Lee was in perfect physical condition, so the sudden collapse and brain swelling were very unusual.

Lee then began to lose weight, much to the consternation of his friends, who urged him to see his doctor again. But he seemed too wrapped up in his work – this was the break he had dreamed of for so long. Two months after his check-up, Lee was working on a script in the Hong Kong apartment of Betty Ting-pei, his co-star, when he suddenly complained of a bad headache. The actress offered Lee an Equagesic painkiller – a two-layer tablet containing aspirin, calcium carbonate, and ethoheptazine citrate. The drug had been prescribed for Ting-pei by her doctor. Lee took the tablet and said he was going for a nap in the actress's bed. He never woke up again. At 9.30pm, Raymond Chow arrived at the apartment to pick the film star up for a dinner engagement. When he found he could not wake Lee, he called for a doctor, whose efforts to revive him were in vain. Bruce Lee was pronounced dead at Queen Elizabeth Hospital. The world was rocked by the news.

The circumstances surrounding Lee's death were interpreted as suspicious by many. Lee had not been taken to the nearest hospital when he was found unconscious, and traces of cannabis were found in his dead body. Many wondered how someone regarded as 'the fittest man in the world' could just die without any apparent cause. A coroner's inquest was convened on 3 September, which uncovered two important findings. Firstly, the amount of cannabis found in Lee's body was too small to have contributed to the actor's death. Secondly, Lee had 'probably' died because of a hypersensitivity to a compound in the painkiller he took – possibly the aspirin component. The official verdict was 'death by misadventure'. Case closed.

But several unsavoury facts were bandied about by the media regarding Lee's behaviour on the eve of his death. It was learned that Lee had publicly attacked Lo Wei – the man who directed *The Big Boss* and other kung fu genre films – on the very day before he died. But the incident was quickly put down to being the climax of a long-standing feud between the two men. There were also rumours that the Chinese Mafia and the Triads had a hand in the actor's demise, and there were other exotic theories gleaned from people who had been close to the star. For instance, it came to light that during the last months of Lee's life, certain mysterious, nameless individuals had approached him and told him he was surrounded by 'bad omens'. Some believed these 'men in black' to be members of an obscure Eastern sect who had come to America to warn Lee about flaunting the closely-guarded secrets of the ancient fighting arts. These alleged visitors were said to have killed Lee with the 'death-touch' or 'dim mak' as it is known in the Far East.

According to legend, a person who is trained in dim mak can dispose of his enemy by applying the briefest of pressures on the non-critical points of the victim's body. The victim does not die immediately, but succumbs after a length of time has passed. The delay period is governed by the particular nerve-points that are chosen and the amount of pressure applied to each point. It is easy to scoff at such a concept of killing by touch, but there are historical records which state that the art of dim mak was in use during the T'ang Dynasty (AD 618-906), and in Taiwan, even today, the deadly art is still alleged to be employed for the execution of 'perfect murders'.

The reports of Lee losing weight shortly before he died have led some students of the Eastern arts to conclude that the actor was killed by a lethal technique known as 'duann mie', which, without going into too much esoteric detail, is a way of killing an enemy by directing a blow against a specific vein, which leads to a wasting away of the victim through the ensuing disruption of specific blood vessels. Oddly enough, when Bruce Lee's body was examined by a pathologist, the blood vessels in the lungs were found to be unaccountably damaged in a way described by the medical expert as 'strange'.

EDGAR ALLAN POE
Did the Master of the Macabre Murder the Cigar Girl?

In July 1841, the body of Mary Rogers, a 21-year-old brunette, was found in the Hudson River at New Jersey. She had been sexually assaulted, and her hands had been tied behind her back. She had also been strangled with a piece of lace.

Mary Rogers had been the only daughter of a respectable widow who ran a boarding-house for clerks in New York. in her teens, she was known as the 'cigar girl' at John Anderson's tobacconist shop on Broadway. Her beauty, and soft, almost child-like voice made her very popular with the clientele, and she received a lot of male attention. And yet, Mary was unaffected by her good looks, and had an irreproachable reputation for chastity and veracity.

In October 1838, she went missing, without warning, for an entire week. When she reappeared, she told her boss, Mr Anderson, that she had been 'tired' and had been staying with her Aunt during the missing period. However, it was later discovered that the girl had been seduced by an officer of the US Navy, and kept at Hoboken for a week. And while she was at Hoboken, people had reported seeing her with another man who was described as a tall individual with a dark complexion. Mary never revealed the identity of the other man.

About a week after she returned to Anderson's store, Mary decided to leave her job. She returned to her mother's boarding-house and took up a job there. One of the lodgers at the house, Daniel Payne, found her irresistible. She reciprocated his affection, and soon they became engaged.

Mary gently tapped on Daniel's door on the morning of 25 July 1841. When Daniel answered, his fiancée told him she was going to spend the day with Mrs Downing, her aunt, and she asked Daniel to collect her later in the evening. But Daniel forgot to pick her up.

The next day, Daniel, realising his mistake, called on Mrs Downing but she said that her niece hadn't visited her. On Wednesday, the body of Mary Rogers was found floating in the waters of Hudson Bay. She had been mutilated and strangled. A piece of lace torn from her dress hung about her neck. A post-mortem revealed that the girl had been raped repeatedly – possibly by up to six men, according to the coroner. Mary's battered face was barely recognisable, and her shoulders and loins were black and yellow with severe bruising.

When Daniel Payne was informed of his fiancée's death, he went into a state of shock and committed suicide a few weeks later. The police had considered Payne as a suspect, but they also suspected two other people: Joseph Morse, a wood engraver who had been noticed eyeing Mary in a lustful way, and William Kucuck, a sailor, who had once lodged at the boarding-house. Morse was cleared when a young woman came forward who said she had been with him on the day that Mary Rogers had been missing. Kucuck had no alibi, but the police decided that he had no motive for the murder and he too was released.

John Anderson, Mary's former employer, was also grilled by the police, but he had a concrete alibi. The murder investigation seemed to have reached a dead end, when the coroner on the case received a letter from an anonymous man. The writer of the missive claimed that he had seen Mary arrive by boat at Bull's Ferry, Hoboken on the fateful Sunday. She was in the company of six rough-looking men, and seemed to be flirting with them in a sexually provocative manner. She entered the nearby woods with the men, laughing and singing. Another boat had arrived minutes later carrying a trio of distinguished, well-dressed gentlemen. These three men got off the boat, approached two bystanders, and asked them what the woman was doing in the company of so many uncouth louts. The anonymous letter-writer didn't hear what the bystanders said in reply.

The New York and New Jersey police worked long and hard on the evidence contained in the letter, without any success, but the course of the investigation took a dramatic turn when the two bystanders came forward to corroborate the details of the anonymous letter. More witnesses then came forward. A driver who had been in the area of Hoboken that Sunday said he had seen Mary Rogers with a tall, well-dressed gentleman going into a road-house near the Elysian Fields summer resort. The road-house was called Nick Mullen's.

The police lost no time in taking up this new lead. They interviewed the road-house keeper, a Mrs Loss, and she confirmed the driver's story. She said Mary and the mysterious tall dark stranger had eaten a meal together, then left the road-house and were seen entering the local woods. Mrs Loss and several people present later heard a scream coming from the woods. Around this time, two watchmen said they also heard the sounds of a woman moaning somewhere in the woodland.

Some days later, Mrs Loss's children were playing in the woods when they found Mary's petticoat, parasol, silk scarf and handkerchief in a thicket. Again, the case reached a cul-de-sac, and the police finally admitted defeat.

Eighteen months later, the case became immortalised in a detective story by one of the world's most famous writers – Edgar Allan Poe, master of the macabre. He called his story *The Mystery of Marie Roget* – and he set his version of the Mary Rogers murder case in Paris. In the tale, Poe's brilliant, wry detective, Dupin, quickly reconstructs the events which led to the brutal murder of the young woman. He discredits the coroner's findings of gang-rape, and asserts that the killer was in fact a lone assassin. He easily deduces this fact by pointing out that there were signs of a struggle at the scene of the crime in the woods, but if six men had been involved, as the police had said, then they would have easily overpowered the girl, and there would be no indications of any struggle whatsoever. Dupin eventually gets to a point in the story where he is about to name the murderer, when Poe irritatingly uses a literary diversion to end the story by pretending he is the editor of the magazine, thus censoring the climactic denouement.

However, it now looks as if Edgar Allan Poe might not have been using the false censorship gimmick as a literary trick at all. He may well have used it to avoid implicating himself in the murder of Mary Rogers. In the light of recent evidence, it seems that Poe's amazingly realistic story detailing Marie Roget's demise is based on facts that could have only been known to the murderer of the real life victim, Mary Rogers. And Poe may have been that man.

In the summer of 1841, the imaginative 32-year-old writer was in an alcoholic limbo, drinking continuously to ease the stress he was experiencing over the slow death of his wife Virginia, who was in the final throes of consumption. According to Poe himself he was insane during this traumatic period and 'suffered long fits of absolute unconsciousness'. He would often seek refuge from his trouble by going into the local woods.

According to several reliable reports, Poe, who was a frequent visitor to New York, actually visited Anderson's tobacconist's on 3 October 1838, and became infatuated with the ravishing, porcelain-skinned cigar girl. Could Poe have been the tall, dark-complexioned man who Mary was seen talking to at Hoboken when she went missing for the first time in October 1838? And was he also the man of the same description who left the road-house with Mary Rogers for the woods on the day on which she was mercilessly battered to death after a repeated, unusually brutal rape? The horror writer certainly fits the bill. He was tall for the time – about five feet nine inches, with an olive complexion.

If Poe did kill Mary Rogers, why did he feel the need to write about his vile deed? Did he get some perverted pleasure out of it? Poe's books are populated by sick, egocentric sadists, and the writer often told acquaintances that the death of the desirable women in his stories never failed to give him 'a poetic thrill'.

At the age of 40, Poe – by this time a drunk and a drug addict – lay panting on his deathbed feverishly whispering, "Lord help my poor soul," over and over again until he died.

DANIEL DUNGLAS HOME
The Victorian Sorcerer Scientists Could Not Discredit

Daniel Dunglas Home was born near Edinburgh on 20 March 1833. His father, William Home, was the illegitimate son of Alexander, tenth Earl of Home, who died in 1841. Little is known of Daniel's early life, but when he was four, the eighth child of the Home family started to 'see' pictures of future events of which he could not possibly have had any knowledge. The family showed little surprise at Daniel's gift of second sight, for his mother was herself a clairvoyant descended from a clan of Highland seers. Mr and Mrs Home, who could not afford to feed and clothe their latest child, left him in the care of an aunt, who reared young Daniel until he was nine; at that age Daniel's aunt took him to America to be reunited with his family at Connecticut.

In 1850, 17-year-old Daniel became a convert to the new doctrine of Spiritualism, at a time when the United States was in the grip of a psychic 'contagion'. Three years earlier at Arcadia, New York, two girls – the infamously fraudulent Fox sisters – had sparked a psychical mania after convincing the gullible that spirits of the departed were communicating from the 'other side' by rapping on the walls and furniture of their home. The Fox rappings incident was but the first of a series of widely-reported accounts of supernatural goings-on in New York, which inaugurated the movement of Modern Spiritualism.

The conversion to this controversial movement came about when Daniel Home realised that he possessed a psychic talent which manifested itself in the onset of strange knocking sounds which echoed about his Connecticut home. This naturally frightened his family, but the last straw came when the furniture of the house began to glide about. Daniel's aunt was terrified by the animated chairs and dancing table, and several ministers of religion were called in, but they could not halt the manifestations; the holy men would merely leave after blaming unseen diabolical forces.

The finger of suspicion finally pointed at Daniel. The Home family realised that he was always in the house when the strange phenomenon occurred, and on several occasions his father caught him smirking at the sight of distraught family members being chased by a dining room chair. Enough was enough – the mischievous cynosure was turned out into the street to fend for himself.

He wandered aimlessly for years, staying with friends here and there, but never settling down. Wherever the teenager went, so did the supernatural disturbances, but far from being a nuisance, these psychical commotions proved to be the roaming youth's bread and butter. He gave séances and developed a repertoire that was similar to the stock-in-trade of contemporary spirit mediums. Home would arrange for the guests to sit round a table, he would go into a trance, and soon rappings and spirit voices would pierce the deadly silence. The table would often simultaneously tilt and rise from the floor. But there were several curious aspects to these séances: they were always staged in well-lit rooms (often in the daytime), and they were never held in Home's own house, in contrast to most spiritualists of the day who insisted on holding séances in total darkness, or on their own premises, usually for fraudulent reasons.

When Home returned to Britain in March 1855, he put up at Cox's Hotel in Jermyn Street, London. Home's overt London séances put him in a different league from most of the psychics of his day, but he did have his detractors, the most notable of them being the poet Robert Browning, who loathed the medium. Still, Home had no shortage of eminent admirers, including Queen Victoria, Charles Dickens, Lord Lytton, William Makepeace Thackeray, John Ruskin and Elizabeth Barrett Browning.

By this stage in his career, Home had added levitation, apports (disembodied hands that dissolve after materialisation), and bodily elongation to his routine. An early account of his gravity-defying ability reads:

I had hold of his hand at the time, and I felt his feet – they were lifted a foot from the floor! Again and again he was taken from the floor; and the third time he was carried to the lofty ceiling of the apartment, with which his hand and head came into gentle contact.

On another occasion, Home flew into the house of a Mr SC Hall (at 15 Ashley Place) via an open window on the third floor. Mr Hall recoiled in terror at the sight, then watched in disbelief as Home floated around the room like a soap bubble, before skimming out through the open window again. He came to earth with a slight jolt a few yards away from Hall's home. Mr Hall excitedly told the first caller to the house, a Mrs Henrietta Ward, about Home's flight, and he declared, "I don't doubt the day when he will float around St Paul's!"

Between the years 1855 and 1864 Home travelled around Europe, performing at the courts of Holland, France, Russia and Prussia. His series of séances in the Tuilleries in Paris greatly impressed Napoleon III and the Empress Eugénie, and he even received an audience with the Pope. In 1859, he married a god-daughter of the Tsar, a beautiful young lady, charming and possessed of means, but she died four years later.

In 1871, the multi-talented physicist and chemist, Sir William Crookes, investigated Home. Crookes subjected the famed medium to a number of tests, beginning with a simple experiment designed to measure his alleged ability to move objects at a distance (telekinesis). Crookes asked the psychic to move a spring balance at the end of the room. Home achieved this easily, which shocked and intrigued Crookes. The scientist then instructed Home to sit at a table under which a closed copper cage was situated. The cage contained an accordion, which Crookes asked Home to play using his telekinetic powers. Home obliged. The accordion played by itself, even though it was untouched by human hands. It continued to play even when Home moved away from the table.

Home also gave a startling demonstration of his immunity to fire. He reached into an open fire in front of Crookes and stirred the burning coals with his hand. He then picked up a piece of red-hot coal – 'as big as an orange' according to Crookes – and proceeded to blow on it until it became white-hot. He later put the incandescent lump of coal back onto the fire and when Crookes examined Home's hand, he was baffled to find that the medium had suffered no burns whatsoever.

Crookes carried out more tests, and later made a list of the strange phenomena he had experienced while investigating Home. He catalogued the following:

- *Unaccountable movement of heavy bodies with contact, but without physical pressure.*
- *Currents of air.*
- *Changes of temperature (registered on a thermometer).*
- *Percussive noises – sometimes raps, but sometimes faint scratchings, sometimes detonations.*
- *Alteration in the weight of objects.*
- *Movement of furniture with no contact.*
- *Levitation of furniture with no contact.*
- *Levitation of Home himself.*
- *Movements of articles at a distance.*
- *Tunes on musical instruments while nobody was playing.*
- *Materialisations – I have retained one of these hands in my own. I firmly resolved not to let it escape. There was no struggle or effort made to get loose, but the hand gradually seemed to resolve itself into vapour and faded in that manner from my grasp.*
- *Direct writing – hands, visible or invisible, taking up pens to write messages.*
- *Phantoms.*
- *Demonstrations of intelligence that could not be attributed to the medium: the provision of information, say, about relations of sitters who were no longer alive, and whom Home could have never known.*
- *Translocations – 'apports'.*
- *Points of light darting about and settling on the heads of different persons.*

Crookes evidently forgot to add Home's fire-immunity to the list.

Other scientists of the Victorian age were unwilling to be seen in the same street as Home, let alone in a laboratory with the prodigy. These myopic men of science reasoned that the things which Home allegedly did were simply contrary to the laws of nature, and were therefore quite impossible. But the laws that the sceptical scientists referred to were the old imperial laws of the pre-Einstein, pre-Quantum Theory days of physics, when an atom was thought to be an indivisible billiard ball.

Crookes bravely put his reputation on the line when he published his findings and his paranormal theory of Home, stating that Home's psychic power was '... connected with the human organisation, which for convenience, may be called the Psychic Force'. He was forced to endure the howls of laughter and derision from his colleagues.

At the age of 40, Daniel Dunglas Home went to live in the Mediterranean because of a recurrent tubercular condition, a move which effectively terminated his psychic career. When Home died in 1886, Sir William Crookes, the only scientist who had been bold enough to look into the medium's powers, declared, "He was one of the most lovable of men, whose perfect genuineness and uprightness were beyond suspicion."

Over the years, many researchers have tried to find evidence that detracts from Home's legendary reputation, but it seems as if the lowly-born psychic's claims to fame are faultless. Perhaps researchers should be looking in the opposite, positive direction; instead of concentrating on the demolition of a man who died over a century ago, it would perhaps be more profitable if they opened their minds as Crookes did, in an age when free-thinking was sadly equated with lunacy. In our era of continual technological progress, they should know better; yet there are still scientists who think like their Victorian ancestors.

THE XINJIANG MUMMIES
The Riddle of China's 4000-year-old Caucasian Corpses

Like the civilisations of Sumer, Babylon, Egypt and India, China emerged into prominence along the banks of a great river – in this case, the Hwang-Ho, or Yellow River, which is situated some 200 miles south of Peking. Legendary sources assert that Chinese civilisation began around 2800 BC, but the real date of China's emergence has been more realistically put at 2200 BC.

In those far-off times, tribes from the northern wastes wandered down to the Hwang-Ho valley and settled in the fertile regions to develop an agricultural way of life. It wasn't easy, as the river frequently broke its banks resulting in terrible deluges that wiped out many of the embryonic settlements in a matter of minutes. These catastrophes forced the early communities to join forces in the battle against the elements, and co-operation between the villages and small towns formed the nucleus of Chinese civilisation.

According to the orthodox history books, outsiders had no influence on China's early culture, and Europeans did not visit China until the 16th century, but recently, a discovery was made which should result in the revision of China's history.

In 1987, Victor Mair, Professor of Chinese at the University of Pennsylvania, and his group of students, were touring Urumqi, a Chinese city in the central Asian province of Xinjiang. They decided to visit a museum in the town and in this museum, Professor Mair was astounded to see the recently discovered mummified corpses of a man, a woman, and a child of around the age of two – each clad in purple woollen garments and felt boots. The curator told the professor that the mummies were 3000 years old, but they looked as if they had only just died.

However, what really intrigued Professor Mair wasn't the state of preservation, but the Caucasian features of the corpses. They had blonde hair, long noses, deep-set eyes, and long skulls. The professor was at a loss to explain to his students what these Caucasians could have been doing in ancient China.

It turned out that the three bodies were just a small part of the mystery. More than a hundred other Caucasian mummies had been discovered at sites scattered around the arid foothills of Tian Shan – the 'Celestial Mountains' in the northwest of China, near the borders of the Taklimakan Desert. Buried in the desert, the corpses had become naturally mummified by the searing desert heat which had quickly dried the bodies soon after interment.

Professor Mair was naturally intrigued by the out-of-place cadavers. He had read the ancient Chinese texts that referred to foreigners called the 'Yuezhi' and the 'Wusun' who inhabited China's far western border. The 2nd century texts stated that these people were bellicose barbarians, but it now looks as if these 'barbarians' were, in fact, responsible for bringing the wheel and the secrets of ore smelting to China. Professor Mair was ecstatic about the blonde mummies, but the political turmoil in China which would eventually lead to the Tianamen Square massacre, dissuaded the Pennsylvanian professor from pursuing his investigation. The professor's theory about Caucasians bringing civilisation to China would most certainly have been viewed by the authorities as Western propaganda, so Professor Mair suspended his inquiries and returned home to resume studies of the ancient Chinese texts with a renewed interest.

In September 1991, the world's media reported the discovery of a 5000-year-old corpse that had been found partially preserved up on the icy slopes of the Alps at an altitude of 10,500 feet. The 'Ice Man' had been a Neolithic trader who had apparently died from exposure after being caught in a blizzard during a long journey. The body had been preserved because the wind had dried its tissues and a glacier had later slid over top of it.

When Professor Mair learned of the Ice Man discovery, he was intrigued by the reports of scientists taking DNA samples from the preserved corpse to throw light on the Neolithical man's genetic background. Mair wondered if the same genetic sampling could be carried out on the Xinjiang mummies. He contacted Wang Binghua, the leading archaeologist at Xinjiang who had discovered the first blonde mummies as far back as 1978, and the two men planned another expedition to Qizilchoqa, or the 'Red Hillock' – a location in the northeast of the Xinjiang Province, where the first mummies had been unearthed.

Paolo Francalacci, an anthropological geneticist from the University of Sassari in Italy, travelled with Professor Mair, Wang Binghua and several other experts on a long arduous journey eastward from Urumqi to the mummy site in the summer of

1993. For 30 hours, the researchers endured a bumpy ride in their four-wheel-drive vehicles across hazardous terrain. Finally, after following part of the ancient trading route known as the Silk Road, the rural village of Wupu was sighted. Nearby was the sandy slope of the Red Hillock. Twenty acres on a hill ringed by barbed wire kept the curious at bay. Shallow depressions dotted the slope where the graves of the Caucasians had been uncovered.

Binghua's team started digging first. They excavated to a depth of six feet before coming upon a burial chamber covered with rush matting, wooden logs, and lined with mud bricks. Mair and Francalacci waited tensely as the excavators brought up the first mummy – a blonde male in brightly-coloured woollen clothes. Francalacci wore a face mask and rubber gloves to avoid contaminating the mummy with his own DNA, then took minute samples from the mummy's inner thighs and armpits. He also drew DNA-laden material from its ribs.

Pottery and other everyday items were also found in the burial chamber. Combs, needles made from bone, spindles of thread, fishing hooks, bells, and even loaves of bread were unearthed.

A total of 113 bodies have now been excavated at several sites in Xinjiang, but the mystery of the blonde mummies has still not been resolved. Francalacci is still mystified by the Caucasian DNA samples, and has been comparing his samples with blood and hair samples from people in the Uygur community of Xinjiang. The Uygur have fair hair and complexions, and it is now thought that these people may be the descendants of the Xinjiang mummies.

The garments worn by the ancient Caucasians are also a puzzle. Under a microscope it can be seen that the fibres of the garments are not wool at all, but the outer hair, or kemp, of a goat. The fibres were elaborately dyed green, blue and brown, and woven in a diagonal twill which is more characteristic of tribal garments in ancient Germany and Scandinavia. Furthermore, the complex twill pattern of the clothes indicates that they were woven on a sophisticated loom.

At Subashi, another site where mummies have been found, a woman's grave was found to contain a leather bag. In this bag, archaeologists found knives and medicines made from herbal concoctions. In another grave, a Subashi man's body still displayed the traces of a surgical operation that had been carried out on his neck, with sutures made from horsehair. Professor Mair was enthralled with the find, because he had read in an ancient text of the sophisticated surgical operations performed in China in the 3rd century AD. The codex claimed that doctors of that period administered an anaesthetic to patients that was derived from opium.

The experts still cannot establish where the ancient fair-skinned people came from. Some think they originated on the plains of eastern Europe, and reached

China via the Steppes, but it is only speculation, and evidence to back up this theory is hard to come by.

The Xinjiang mummies have shattered the long-held notion of an ancient China cut off from the rest of the world. Professor Mair insists that, "Influences didn't just flow one way, from China westward."

The majority of the Xinjiang mummies are currently being stored in a damp and inadequately-sized basement at the Institute of Archaeology in Urumqi and they are in danger of disintegrating. Professor Mair has urged China and the West to build a special museum to exhibit the mummies, but the Chinese authorities say they don't have the finance, and as yet, the Western world has shown little interest in preserving the mysterious blonde mummies of Xinjiang.

THE ALENÇON SPACEMAN
The Man Who Fell to Earth in 18th Century France?

There have been many reports of visitors from other planets dropping in on Earth. In 1954, the Japanese authorities detained a man trying to enter the country with a passport that revealed he was from an unheard-of country named 'Taured'. A thorough check was made by the customs officials to determine if there was such a place anywhere on Earth, but they drew a blank. The stranger refused to throw any light on the whereabouts of the mysterious nation of Taured and quickly left Japan.

A similar incident occurred in 1851 when a man calling himself Joseph Vorin was found wandering in the German village of Frankfurt-an-der-Oder. When the German authorities asked the man where he was from, Vorin told them that he was from Laxaria, a country on the continent of Sakria. This baffled the authorities because neither of the places existed anywhere on their map of the world!

In 1905, a young man who was arrested in Paris for stealing a loaf was found to speak an unknown language, and after a lengthy interrogation session, the man managed to convey that he was from a place called Lizbia. Thinking he meant Lisbon, the man was shown a map of Portugal, and a Portuguese interpreter was brought in to talk to him, but it was soon established that the young offender was not from Lisbon. The language the youth spoke was not an invented babble either; it had all the consistent syntactical rules of a language similar to Esperanto. Eventually, the strange-speaking man was released – never to be seen again.

The great student of the unexplained, Charles Fort, once commented on the subject of visitors from other planets:

If there have ever been instances of teleportations of human beings from somewhere else to this Earth, an examination of infirmaries and workhouses and asylums might lead to some marvellous disclosures. Early in the year 1928, a man did appear in a town in New Jersey, and did tell that he had come from the planet Mars. Wherever he came from, everybody knows where he went after telling that.

One of the best documented reports of a possible visitant from another world landing on Earth came from the little French town of Alençon, which is situated about 30 miles north of Le Mans. The town is nowadays famous solely for its fine lace, but over two hundred years ago, Alençon became renowned for something far less mundane.

At around 5am on 12 June 1790, peasants watched in awe as a huge metal sphere descended from the sky, moving with a strange undulating motion. The globe crash-landed onto a hilltop, and the violent impact threw up soil and vegetation which showered the hillside.

The hull of the globe was so hot (possibly from a rocket motor, or because of the rapid descent through the atmosphere) that it ignited the surrounding dry flora, and a grass fire quickly broke out. The peasants rushed up the hillside carrying pails of water, and within a short time, the flames were extinguished.

A large crowd encircled the crashed globe, and some of the more adventurous stepped forward to touch the hull of the unearthly craft to discover that it was quite warm. A physician, two mayors from nearby towns and a number of officials also turned up to see what had descended from the morning sky, and these important witnesses arrived just in time to see something sensational.

A hatch of some sort slid open in the lower hemisphere of the globe, and a man in an outlandish, tight-fitting costume emerged through the hatchway and surveyed the observers with an apprehensive look. He started mumbling something in a strange language and gestured for the crowd to move away from him and his vehicle. A few people stepped back, at which point the man ran through the break in the circle of spectators and fled into the local woods. Some of the peasants also ran away, sensing that something dangerous was about to happen and then the remainder of the crowd decided to follow suit. Seconds after the last members of the crowd had retreated from the sphere, it exploded with a peculiar muffled sound, creating a miniature mushroom-shaped cloud. The debris from the craft sizzled in the grass, and gradually turned to powder.

A police inspector named Liabeuf travelled over a hundred miles from Paris to investigate the crash, and he quizzed many of the witnesses, including the mayors and physician who had been present at the strange spectacle. The inspector organised a thorough search of the woods where the oddly-dressed man had taken refuge, but the hunt resulted in nothing. The stranger seemed to have vanished as mysteriously as he had arrived. In the report to his superiors, Inspector Liabeuf put forward the suggestion that the man who had landed in the globe could have been 'a being from another world' – but the higher authorities in Paris dismissed the intimation as 'a ludicrous idea'.

THE PHANTOM WRITERS
Perplexing Graffiti and Enigmatic Epistles

The earliest mention of mysterious writing is in the Old Testament. In Daniel 5:31, there is an account of strange handwriting that appeared on the wall of Belshazzar's palace on the night of the feast. The mysterious message is interpreted by the prophet Daniel as an omen foretelling the loss of Belshazzar's kingdom. Since those remote times, there have been many more reports of mysterious scrawlings. Some baffling messages have been in the form of graffiti, such as the message left on the wall by Jack the Ripper, which is as incomprehensible today as it was over a century ago, when Jack chalked the words after killing two prostitutes in the early hours of Sunday 30 September 1888. The Whitechapel Murderer's cryptic five-liner declared:

The Juwes are
The men That
Will not be
Blamed for nothing

Another piece of puzzling graffiti greeted the citizens of Owensville, Indiana, on the morning of 7 December 1939. In huge letters on the sidewalk of the public grade school, someone had painted a sentence in huge white letters that read: 'Remember Pearl Harbour!'

A policeman in the town scratched his head as he read the words and said, "Crazy kids. Where is Pearl Harbour, anyway?" No one in the town seemed to know, until two years later, to the day, when an armada of 350 Japanese carrier-launched warplanes attacked the US Pacific Fleet at Pearl Harbour, Hawaii. The Japanese killed 2,330 military personnel and wounded 1,145 in the attack, as well as destroying 247 aircraft, sinking three battleships and eleven warships. But who was the mysterious graffiti writer who had warned the United States of this horrific military assault two years before it happened? No one knows.

Mysterious writing in the form of letters is less common than strange writings on walls, but from time to time there have been reports in the newspapers of malicious chain letters circulating through our cities. These anonymous epistles often instruct the person who opens them to send exact copies of the chain letter to at least three friends, and the abominable letter often says that any failure to duplicate the original missive will result in bad luck or death to the person who has opened the letter. Many of these letters are no doubt sent by people with a warped sense of humour, but some of the senders may be fully-fledged sadists who delight in propagating a wave of dread via the postal system. It will be interesting to see if the computerised version of the chain letter ever traverses the information highways to appear on our home computer and television screens in the near future years.

In 1956, the paranormal researcher Andrew Green was pleasantly surprised to receive a letter from a poltergeist! The letter began: 'Mr Green, Do you remember me? I am Donald ... I took leave to write ... I spoke to you by the glass.' The address at the top of the letter was: 63 Wycliffe Road, Battersea. Green had investigated an alleged poltergeist at that address weeks before, and believed that the writer of the spooky letter was a 15-year-old girl who seemed to be at the epicentre of the supernatural goings-on. But Green couldn't prove his theory; he may well be in possession of the only reported letter written by a poltergeist.

What must surely rank as one of the most bizarre cases of eerie correspondence is the case of the phantom postcard sender which hit the headlines in Britain in 1977. A former councillor and parliamentary candidate, Trevor Silverwood, started receiving postcards at his home in Bridlington, Yorkshire in 1967 – from an irritating nosy parker who told Mr Silverwood about the most trivial details of his private life: what he had eaten for breakfast, what programmes he watched on television, even the colour of his socks. Naturally, Mr Silverwood was a little unnerved by the postcards – which were stamped with postmarks from all over the world, but this soon turned to irritation with the snooper, who continues to plague him to this day. The writing is always in shorthand, and the anonymous correspondent signs the postcards with a little matchstick figure of The Saint – the Leslie Charteris creation. Mr Silverwood is truly baffled by the writer – who posts his annoying messages from India, America, Canada, the Middle East, as well as from cities as near to home as Rotherham and Sheffield.

Shortly before Christmas in 1977, a postcard from Australia arrived at Silverwood's home. One sentence on it read: 'Just for you.' Silverwood told the press: "I would dearly like to get my hands on the Big Brother or Sister who is watching me. It was amusing at first, but now no longer."

As a last resort, Mr Silverwood placed an advertisement in the personal column of his local newspaper, begging the postcard writer to identify himself. A few days later, a postcard arrived from Tenerife which read: 'Don't be naughty. What a nice picture of you the newspaper published!' The anonymous writer was referring to the photograph of Mr Silverwood printed in a national newspaper that included an article on the postcard mystery.

After being questioned by police over a minor driving matter, Mr Silverwood received a postcard from another exotic overseas place that gave a blow-by-blow account of the police questioning, as if the writer was trying to create the impression that he was omniscient.

The identity of the unknown correspondent is still a mystery, as is the identity of a similar correspondent who changed the course of British politics in the 18th century. This correspondent wrote under several pseudonyms, penning his first satirical letter in 1767, but from January 1769 to January 1772, he wrote 70 vicious but brilliant letters under the pen-name 'Junius'; even the mere mention of the name induced feelings of terror and dread in the corrupt circles of the British élite.

All of the letters appeared in the *Public Advertiser* in London. The first one, printed in the popular readers' letters column on 21 January 1769, accused the Prime Minister of being a gambler. The libellous sentence in the scathing letter read: 'The finances of a nation, sinking under its debts and expenses, are committed to a young nobleman already ruined by play.'

In December 1769, Junius criticised King George III. In the seditious letter, Junius warned the monarch of the dire repercussions that could result from the oppression of the Irish and the Americans, and audaciously reminded the king of the execution of Charles I. Junius ended the caustic criticism with a sentence about the king that shocked every reader: 'While he plumes himself upon the security of his title to the crown, he should remember that, as it was acquired by one revolution, it may be lost by another.'

The printer of the *Public Advertiser*, Henry Woodfall, was promptly arrested on a charge of seditious libel, but the jury refused to convict him, and he was soon released.

The letters from Junius ended in early 1772. Junius, whoever he was, had single-handedly exposed the corruption that was rife in the upper echelons of 18th century London. His razor-sharp pen cut down the corrupt king himself, his fawning hypocritical bigwigs, and the mercenary Members of Parliament whose only incentive for entering the House of Commons was to make a killing for themselves. Junius opened the eyes of the common man to the rotten hierarchy of the king and his Government, and because of him, newspapers were allowed to report Parliamentary debates, and those in power remained under the close scrutiny of the press.

For over two centuries, historians have argued over the identity of Junius. All that is known is that he was obviously an ardent Whig partisan of the Grenville faction and a fierce opponent of the administrations of the Duke of Grafton and Lord North. Over a hundred people have been suspected of writing the Junius letters, the most likely candidates being Edmund Burke, the Irish philosopher, politician and orator, and Sir Philip Francis, a politician and pamphleteer, who was a clerk in the War Office in 1762. Of these two suspects, Francis emerged as the prime one in 1963, when Alvar Ellegard, a Swedish linguistics expert, put copies of the Junius letters and handwriting samples of Sir Philip Francis through a mainframe computer. The results of the computerised text analysis apparently convinced Ellegard that Junius was Sir Philip. But many historians disagreed with the results, so we'll probably never know the true identity of the most feared social critic in the history of British politics. This is precisely what Junius smugly predicted shortly before the letters ceased when he wrote: 'I am the sole depository of my secret, and it shall die with me.'

,   # BILL FROST
The Welsh Carpenter Who Flew Before the Wright Brothers

In the early years of the 20th century, one of man's oldest dreams was finally realised: the dream of manned flight. History records that Orville and Wilbur Wright made the first powered and controlled flights on 17 December 1903, at Kitty Hawk, North Carolina. Their first flight was ground-breaking enough, but the second one lasted 59 seconds before their propeller-driven glider came to earth 250 metres from the take-off point – quite an achievement in those times. The two aviation pioneers were subsequently hailed as heroes, and were able to abandon their cycle business for more lucrative enterprises.

Wilbur shipped the aircraft to France, where it was passionately received as a modern wonder of the world, and in 1909, Orville secured a contract to supply the US Army with his planes. It was a real American success story. But unknown to the Wright brothers, a humble Welsh carpenter named Bill Frost had already taken to the skies in a powered, heavier-than-air, flying machine, some eight years before the historical flights at Kitty Hawk.

It all began around 1868 when 20-year-old Bill Frost was working on the building of Hean Castle – an absurd Victorian folly. As the youth was carrying a 12-foot-long pine plank along scaffolding, a sudden fierce gust of wind rushed up under him and propelled the plank – and Frost – into the air. The carpenter landed gently, still clinging to the plank – and that aeolian incident fired his youthful imagination. From that moment on he was continually preoccupied with finding a way to invade the domain of the birds and clouds.

The people of Saundersfoot, the village in the west of Wales where Frost lived, laughed at his dream, just as the dullards of long ago had laughed at the futile flight attempts of Leonardo da Vinci and the dangerous balloon escapades of the Montgolfier brothers. Even the men that were to go down in the official history of flight – the Wright brothers – were initially regarded as fools. For hours, the brothers would watch gannets gliding through the sky and imitate the birds by stretching out and tilting their arms. This provided ample amusement for the coastguards who used to watch the seemingly crazy, would-be aeronauts. So Bill Frost was in good company when he ran down Stammers Hill, entrapped within hopelessly inadequate aerofoil designs, while onlookers smiled and laughed scornfully. It was always the same outcome – the 19th century Icarus demoralised and breathless at the bottom of Stammers Hill, as those content to remain on terra firma gloated at the antics of the 'Bird Man'.

But Bill Frost learned from his mistakes, and possessed a vision that was decades ahead of its time – a vision of a flying machine that could be driven by two propellers revolving horizontally, which would provide lift in a way similar to the Harrier jump jet. But because the poor carpenter had no one to approach for advice in his isolated village, and had no books to help him, most of the blueprints for his wonder machine stayed in his head, until he eventually managed to save and borrow enough money to patent the aeroplane in 1894.

In September of the following year, the Bird Man of Stammer Hill took off in his prototype plane from the field of his father-in-law, Fred Watkins. The strange-looking contraption buzzed through the warm evening air over Stammers Hill, and soared over the heads of the people who had previously laughed at Bill Frost's gravity-defying attempts. None of them laughed now. They surveyed the 48-year-old flying man slanting across the coppery-coloured clouds. The children below squealed with delight at the aerobat, but a storm suddenly roared in from Cardigan Bay which shook the plane violently. Frost started to lose altitude. The plane nose-dived, then levelled off, but continued to lose height. It scudded low over the fields until its undercarriage smashed into the top branches of an ash tree. Frost was incredibly lucky to survive the first ever aircrash, as the plane was wrecked beyond repair. The people who had observed the stomach-turning descent came running to the crash-site to take a look at the strange machine's remains. Some still scoffed at the fallen pilot, despite his incredible achievement.

With no money to rebuild his plane, Frost decided to offer his patent to the War Office. He expected a substantial financial return, but instead, he received a letter from the Under Secretary of State, William St John Broderick, which declared: 'This Nation does not intend to adopt aerial navigation as a means of warfare.'

For years, Bill Frost told anyone who would listen that manned flight would soon change the face of war, travel and commerce – but few took his predictions seriously. In his last years he realised he was slowly becoming blind, and ultimately became a familiar, pathetic-looking character in the village, led about by two goats.

With tears in his dying eyes, the Welsh visionary smiled and pointed skywards in the early days of World War One, when he heard the drone of three German airships looming in the clouds, high over Pembrokeshire.

"Look!" he shouted, "I said they could do it. Look!"

THE MAGI
Who Were the Wise Men from the East?

Every year, a certain star is depicted on millions of Christmas cards all over the world. It is sung about in carols, it shines down from the tops of Christmas trees, and foil imitations of it twinkle over Nativity scenes; but just what was the Star of Bethlehem? Is it just a myth, or did the starry messenger really exist in the skies of Judaea? And who were the Three Wise Men who are said to have followed the mysterious star? Well, let us analyse these two intriguing features of Christmas lore separately. We'll begin with the Star of Bethlehem. For centuries, theologians and scientists have argued over their interpretations of the celestial event, which was recorded only by the apostle Matthew. In the second chapter of his gospel, Matthew tells us:

Now, when Jesus was born in Bethlehem of Judaea in the days of Herod the King, behold, there came wise men from the East to Jerusalem, saying, "Where is he that is born king of the Jews? For we have seen his star in the East and have come to worship him."

According to Matthew, Herod summoned these Wise Men and told them that if they happened to find the newborn king, they had to divulge the child's whereabouts to him. Later, the Wise Men saw the guiding star in the Eastern sky and it led them to the little stable where the baby Jesus slept.

In the 17th century, the great German astronomer Kepler sent shockwaves through the Christian world when he suggested that the star which the Wise Men had followed might have been nothing more than a conjunction of the planets Saturn and Jupiter. However, it is now known that no such conjunctions were visible in the skies over the Holy Land during the period that St Matthew mentions – around 5 or 6 BC, according to the estimates of historical scholars.

After Kepler's heretical attempts to explain away the Star of Bethlehem as a natural phenomenon, many other scientists also tried to rationalise the stellar oddity. Halley's Comet was cited as one interpretation, but astronomers have calculated that the comet had already visited and left the heavens ten years before Christ's birth.

Another theory proposed that the star which hovered over the stable was actually a distant star that had exploded or gone 'supernova', to use astronomers' jargon. Such stellar cataclysmic explosions do occur from time to time, and can be bright enough to be seen in the blue daytime skies for months. It is recorded in ancient Chinese astronomical texts that a supernova of this class of magnitude did occur around 4 BC. Chinese astronomers of the time recorded that a star flared up in the constellation of Aquila the Eagle, just below the bright star Altair, and what's more, it has now been computed that, to anyone standing at the South Gate of Jerusalem, the brilliant star would have appeared to be over Bethlehem.

AJ Morehouse, an American scientist who uncovered the Chinese record, believes that the Star of Bethlehem is still in the sky, albeit very faint. Opponents of Morehouse's theory have pointed out that the supernova of 4 BC occurred too late to be associated with the birth of Christ.

Another problem with Morehouse's hypothesis is that if the Star of Bethlehem was a supernova, surely such a bright spectacle in the night sky would not have gone unnoticed by the inhabitants of Judaea? Moreover, a supernova cannot simply hover in the sky as the Star of Bethlehem was said to have done over the manger. Like every other celestial object, a supernova, however bright, will steadily move westward. So, despite all the conjecture and historical research, we are still no nearer to uncovering the truth about the most enigmatic herald in history.

Just as enigmatic as the star are the Three Wise Men who followed it. Who were they? Matthew simply states that they were from the East, without specifying which country, and contrary to popular belief, he does not say that they were kings, nor that there were three of them. There are four kings on the 4th century frescoes in the Roman catacombs of St Peter and St Marcellinus, and four on the 3rd century catacomb frescoes at St Domitilla. Some mediaeval versions of the Nativity have twelve Magi!

Were the Wise Men Gentiles? Most Biblical historians believe that the visitors to Bethlehem were most probably Babylonian Jews, but every culture has had its own theories about the Wise Men. When Matthew said the sages were from the 'East', he was talking about a vague region stretching from Aleppo in the north-west to present-day Mosul in Iraq, which means there is a possibility that the Wise Men were not Jewish at all.

Were the Gentiles expecting a saviour? In his fourth *Eclogue*, the Roman poet Virgil (who died 19 years before Christ's birth) records the widespread expectation that a messianic-like individual in the not-too-distant future would come to rule a peaceful world. Virgil mentions that the birth of this long-awaited ruler of the Earth will be presaged by 'a Golden Race which will spring up throughout the world'. Curiously, the Roman poet also says that a 'Virgin Lady' will figure in the new scheme of things. So, it would seem that the Gentiles were also awaiting the arrival of a saviour.

Another Gentile people who have been connected with the Wise Men are the Medes, an ancient race which settled in the vicinity of the Caspian Sea and established the nation of Media. In the 7th century BC, the Medes spread south until they reached the fringes of Elam on the east of the lower Tigris. Among the Medes, there were members of a priestly caste credited with amazing occult powers, who followed the teachings of the Perso-Iranian prophet Zarathustra, whose commandments were, 'Good thoughts, good words, good deeds'.

These Medean occultists were known by the name now synonymous with the Wise Men of the Bible: the Magi. 'Magi' is the plural form of the word 'magus' which means 'sorcerer'. The Magi were identified with astrology, oneirology (the study of dreams), and the practice of the 'hidden science', (also known as the Ancient Science) or the occult.

For centuries, the Medeans have been associated with the Wise Men, who, tradition claims, were three kings called Melchior, Gaspar and Balthazar. Legend says Melchior brought gold, the emblem of royalty; Gaspar offered frankincense, in token of divinity; and Balthazar gave myrrh – as a symbol of death.

The final resting place of the three kings is said to be Cologne Cathedral, Germany, where a plaque reads:

Having undergone many trials and fatigues for the gospel, the three wise men met at Sewa [Sebaste in Armenia] in AD 54 to celebrate the feast of Christmas. Thereupon, after the celebration of Mass, they died. St Melchior on 1 January aged 116; St Balthazar on 6 January, aged 112; and St Gaspar on 11 January, aged 109.

The alleged remains were discovered in the East in the 4th century and brought from Persia to Constantinople in AD 490 by the Emperor Zeno. The relics later turned up in Milan. When the Holy Roman Emperor Frederick Barbarossa looted Italy in 1164, he took the remains of the three kings from their vault in San Georgio in Milan and gave them to Rainald von Dussel, the Chancellor and Archbishop elect of Cologne. The Emperor told von Dussel that the relics were a reward to the people of Cologne who had backed him in his fight against Pope Alexander III.

However many there were, and whoever they were, most historians agree that the Wise Men were students of astrology, which was very popular among the Jewish communities of the Levant at that time. Among the timeworn Hebrew and Aramaic texts of the Dead Sea Scrolls (which were discovered in 1947) there are astrological charts depicting the signs of the Zodiac and mystical passages (that read like modern-day horoscopes) referring to the influence of the stars and planets on the newly-born.

ELIZABETH CANNING
The Teenager Who Divided a Nation

On the night of 1 January 1753, 18-year-old Elizabeth Canning went missing. Earlier on that New Year's Day she had left her employer, Mr Lyon, who ran a carpentry business in the City of London, telling him she was going to visit her mother. Elizabeth did see her mother, and she also paid a visit to her Uncle Folley who lived near the London Docks, and he made such a fuss of his favourite niece that she didn't get away from his home until 10pm, and even then, he insisted he would have to accompany her on her homeward journey to Aldermanbury Street in the City. Her uncle and aunt escorted the teenager as far as Houndsditch, a mere ten-minute walk from her home, when Elizabeth said she would be alright from there on, and after kissing her, Uncle Folley reluctantly turned and headed home with his wife.

Over an hour later, Elizabeth's mother, Bet, a widow with five children, stood on her doorstep, waiting anxiously to catch sight of her overdue daughter. As midnight came and went, Mrs Canning began to fear her eldest daughter had been abducted or even murdered. The people of Aldermanbury Street quickly came to Bet Canning's aid. The neighbours made a collection to finance a reward for anyone who could provide information about the girl's whereabouts. Some of the collected money paid for a 'missing' advert that was printed in the local press. The advert gave a description of Elizabeth and offered a two-guinea reward for information leading to her discovery. But four weeks passed without any news of the teenager.

Then, out of the blue, on 29 January, Elizabeth Canning turned up at Aldermanbury Street, limping and half naked. A bloodstained piece of torn cloth was tied around her head, and she sported a nasty gash on her left ear.

She hobbled into her house, where her mother threw her arms around her battered and bruised daughter. She sat her down at the table.

"Oh dear! What happened to you? Who did this? Who did it?" cried Bet.

Elizabeth explained how, soon after leaving Uncle Folley, she had been brutally set upon by a couple of burly rogues. One of the scoundrels hit her on the head with a cosh, knocking her unconscious. They ripped off her dress and apron and stole her half-guinea. When Elizabeth came round, she was being dragged along the ground, but was too weak to resist. She was taken into a house and thrown at the feet of an old woman. In her dazed state she noticed that two younger women were also present, and looked down at Elizabeth, grinning.

"Why don't you go our way m'dear?" the old woman leered at Elizabeth. The kidnapped girl felt terror in the pit of her stomach as she realised that the old woman was asking her to become a prostitute. The place she had been dragged to was a brothel.

Elizabeth felt her sticky, bloody head wound and cried, "No! Let me go!"

The old woman produced a knife and cut the laces of Elizabeth's corset. She slapped the weeping girl's face. Then, grabbing hold of her, she forced her upstairs to a dismal-looking room, where the terrified girl remained a prisoner for four weeks, with only a mouldy loaf of bread and a pitcher of water had been left for her. Almost freezing to death before the empty fire grate, the teenager finally decided to make an escape attempt. As quietly as she could, she yanked down the hard wooden boards that were nailed across the window. She scrambled out onto the penthouse roof and noiselessly dropped into the secluded street. Strengthened by her desperation, she then made the arduous ten-mile journey home, nervously looking behind her all the time.

"Where was this place?" Bet asked, shaking with anger.

"Hertford Road, mother," replied Elizabeth knowingly, basking in the comfort and warmth of the fire and the security of her home.

Mrs Canning was later telling her neighbour Robert Scarratt about Elizabeth's ordeal, when he said that he knew the road well.

"I'll lay a guinea to a farthing that the house where Liz was kept was the brothel that Mother Wells runs," he said. "Aye, she's a gypsy."

Elizabeth seemed to confirm his conclusion, saying that she had heard the surname Wells, or possibly Wills, mentioned at the house.

The news of the girl's terrible ordeal quickly travelled the length of Aldermanbury Street, and a mob of incensed citizens immediately set out for the house of Mother Wells, taking Elizabeth with them.

The mood of the crowd grew angrier during the ten-mile journey to the house and, on arrival, several members hammered on the door. Mother Wells herself answered and was roughly pushed aside as the vengeful multitude poured into the alleged house of ill-repute. They found a dark room upstairs which seemed to be the one described by poor Elizabeth. There was hay on the floor, a water pitcher, a cask, and a saddle. But there was no sign of the fire grate that Elizabeth had mentioned, and no penthouse roof outside the window which Elizabeth claimed to have climbed on during her escape.

Elizabeth was taken to the house, where she identified the room where she had been kept a prisoner. Downstairs, Mother Wells and Mary Squire, another old gypsy, were spat on by the mob, even though the two women professed to be baffled by the invasion of their home. Elizabeth came downstairs and pointed to Mary Squires.

"That's the old woman that robbed me," she said.

"Eh?" frowned Mary Squires, apparently shocked at the girl's accusation. "When did I rob you?"

"On New Year's Day!" screamed Elizabeth.

"Impossible. On that day I was a hundred and twenty miles away," Mary Squires replied.

The other inhabitants of the house stood by, frightened by the hubbub and the irate mob. Mary Squire's daughter, Lucy, and her young friend, a beautiful blonde prostitute named Virtue Hall, were naturally suspected of being the two young women whom Elizabeth had mentioned in her story, and Mary's thick-set son

George was assumed to be one of the despicable brutes who had attacked and abducted young Liz. The five suspects were taken to the house of the local magistrate. Mother Wells and Mary Squires were charged and taken to jail, the entire time loudly protesting their innocence.

Four days later, Virtue Hall was brought before Henry Fielding, the novelist and playwright, who was also London's first police magistrate. Fielding interrogated Hall in such a severe manner that she was reduced to tears, and she finally agreed to tell Fielding all she knew about the Canning incident. The prostitute offered details about Elizabeth Canning having been brought to Mother Wells's house by two gypsies, but before Hall could provide further details, Fielding was accused of bullying the prostitute just to extract the statement he wanted.

When Mother Wells and Mary Squires went on trial a fortnight later, the latter called three witnesses to prove that she had been in Abbotsbury, Dorset, on the day the alleged abduction took place. But the jury simply refused to believe her and the two gypsy women were later found guilty. Squires was sentenced to death by hanging, but Mother Wells was given part of her punishment immediately, before the court. An incandescent branding iron was brought in and she was held still by two men as the branding iron was pressed against her hand. She let out a horrible scream which was swamped by the cheering of the court spectators; she fainted and was taken away to Newgate prison to begin a six-month sentence.

British justice had been done – or had it? Sir Crispe Gascoyne, London's Lord Mayor, did not think so. He thought the trial had been a totally biased travesty of justice and wrote to the vicar of Abbotsbury, asking him to question the three witnesses who had been produced at the court for the defence. The vicar replied that the men in question were honest and trustworthy citizens who still maintained that the condemned Mary Squires had been with them on New Year's Day.

Virtue Hall was also questioned by Gascoyne, and she nervously admitted that she had given false evidence to avoid going to prison herself. Gascoyne immediately visited Mother Wells in her cell, and after questioning the old woman about the events of that fateful New Year's Day, he was satisfied that Wells and Squires were victims of a gross miscarriage of justice. Thanks to his diligent efforts, Squires was pardoned just one day before the execution date, and Mother Wells was also released.

By now, the nation was divided by the Canning affair. The 'Canningites' believed that Wells and Squires had kept Elizabeth Canning imprisoned, whilst the 'Egyptians' (thus called because it was commonly held that gypsies were descended from the Egyptians) maintained that Elizabeth Canning was an evil liar. In May 1754, the Egyptian campaigners managed to convince the authorities that

Elizabeth Canning had been somewhat economical with the truth, and the teenager was indicted for perjury.

She was found guilty and transported on 31 July 1754. What became of her is a mystery, and just what actually had happened on that New Year's Day in 1753 has never been explained. Was she abducted, or did she invent the incident? If she did, how can we account for her injuries, and where did she stay for those four weeks? The Canning affair has never been fully explained and still remains a perplexing case.

REYNARD BECK
The Man Who Could Fly

Dream researchers – or oneirologists, as they are officially known – say that the most commonly reported dream in every culture is the dream of unaided flight. In this sleep fantasy, the dreamer takes to the air and soars above trees and buildings in a state of ecstasy. But unaided flight is just a dream, surely?

For centuries there have been tales of Eastern gurus and other holy and mystical men of the world who have allegedly been capable of levitation, but scientists are very sceptical about reports of people overcoming the laws of gravity, although the late scientist and science fiction writer, Isaac Asimov, claimed that one day in the not-too-distant future, men would be able to fly under their own power on the moon – under pressurised domes. An Earth-dweller on the moon would only weigh one-sixth of his terrestrial weight, thus allowing anyone with even rudimentary strap-on wings to fly through the air. Asimov stresses that if the common lunar gas Argon was mixed with the dome's atmosphere, the resulting denser air would make flying even easier.

But here in this world, in the state of Missouri in June 1884, there was a report of one man who could resist the gravitational pull that makes us all prisoners of the Earth.

In the pastoral town of Dexter, near the Mississippi River, there lived a 27-year-old farm-worker named Reynard Beck. Reynard and his elder brother Samuel worked the small farm for their widowed mother. After the death of Sam Beck senior in 1879, the Beck family had a rough time trying to make enough money to live decently. The family enjoyed the utmost respect from their neighbours, who admired the way the proud Becks refused help from anybody, but their integrity meant that the Becks had virtually no social life at all. Sam and Reynard could not even afford the most basic pleasures in life like good clothes or the occasional drink. In fact, both boys were unable to court girls because of their financial position, but they plodded on, content with what little they had.

One morning, before the sun was up, Mrs Beck called her sons to breakfast. Reynard awoke to the aroma of eggs and bacon, yawned, rubbed the sleep from his eyes, then suddenly experienced an intense feeling of euphoria – and a sensation of weightlessness. He threw back his blankets and was about to get out of bed when he started to float up towards the ceiling. He wasn't at all frightened – just amazed. He felt as light as a feather, and assumed he must be dreaming. The farmer reached out and grabbed hold of the headboard of his bed and pulled himself down onto the mattress in a state of disbelief.

Mrs Beck shouted to her son again and told him that his breakfast was going cold. Reynard reacted by letting go of the headboard, hoping that the weightlessness had subsided – but it hadn't – and he found himself floating slowly upward again like a soap bubble. He ended up spread-eagled against the ceiling, where he remained, wondering at the incredible thing that had happened to him. What had caused it? He knew he was about 200 pounds in weight, so how could he just float? Naturally, he was baffled. He pressed the soles of his bare feet against the ceiling and pushed them hard, propelling himself down towards the bed. Before he could rise again, he grabbed the bed's headboard and pulled himself down onto the mattress once again. He then took hold of a chair and clutched it against his chest. The weight of the chair was just sufficient to keep him grounded. Reynard ignored his mother's impatient cries and slowly moved toward the chest where his clothes were kept. He opened a drawer and took out an old leather belt that he wore for fishing. Attached to this belt were various lead weights he used on his fishing rod. Reynard wedged his feet under the chest, put the belt on, and was relieved to find that the weighted belt kept his feet firmly on the floor.

Reynard was a God-fearing, superstitious individual, and avoided telling anyone about his experience in case they accused him of having made a pact with the Devil. So he went down to have breakfast with the weighted belt covered by a loose shirt, and later he worked in the fields without breathing a word to anyone about his strange secret.

Before he went to bed that night, Reynard nervously took off his belt and instantly started to levitate again. At that moment, his brother came into the room and saw him with his hands on the headboard and his feet in the air. He naturally assumed that Reynard was performing a handstand for some reason.

"What on earth are you doin'?" Sam asked, bemused by the vision.

Reynard suddenly lost his grip on the headboard and started rising through the air to the ceiling. Sam stood there, open-mouthed, as he watched his brother bump the ceiling with his head.

"The belt! Hand me the belt, Sam!" shouted Reynard, obviously distressed. Sam picked the weighted belt from the bed and handed it up to his airborne brother.

"How the heck did you do that? That's one neat trick. How on earth did you do it?" Sam asked, suspecting that the amazing feat was performed by wires. But he could see that there were no wires and this truly perplexed him.

As soon as Reynard put the belt back on, he descended again. After he had told his brother how he had woken up to discover his new talent, they both decided to tell their mother, but she seemed more concerned with what people would say about her levitating son, than the mysterious new ability he possessed.

Sam convinced his brother that there was money to be made out of his paranormal ability, and the two men decided to go on the road, exhibiting Reynard as 'The Floating Wonder'.

The act proved to be very popular. When the crowds crushed into the booth to see the show, Reynard simply undid his belt and rose steadily through the air to the canvas roof, where he tethered himself to a metal frame. When news spread of the astounding 'stunt', thousands of people flocked to see the show, and the takings mounted considerably each day.

When the Floating Wonder displayed his anti-gravitational antics at a town in Oklahoma, a few sceptics employed a gang of hooligans to wreck the booth in order to expose what they saw to be the fraudulent goings-on. But the vandals were shocked to discover that no wires or trickery were involved at all. This revelation only served to bolster the growing reputation of the Floating Wonder.

Scientists and doctors turned up at the shows, determined to disprove the myth of the flying farmer, but they soon saw that Reynard Beck was no hoaxer – he really could levitate, but as that went against accepted science, the men of learning refused to comment on the inexplicable gravity-resistant man.

In April 1887, a reporter from the *Kansas Star* was assigned to get to the bottom of the Floating Wonder phenomenon. He later wrote of his attempts to discredit the brothers from Dexter:

Before the exhibition, I thoroughly searched the room, looking for wires, hydraulic ramps, hidden supports – any device that might provide a clue to the mystery, but I found absolutely nothing. While Mr Beck sat in a reclining position three feet from the floor, I beat the air above and below him with a cane, but met no resistance. With the utmost reluctance, I came to the conclusion that he was floating in mid-air.

The Floating Wonder was continually quizzed about the method he employed to leave terra firma, but was unable to offer an explanation. He was as puzzled as everyone else by his unearthly capability. After six years on the road the Beck brothers had netted over one million dollars from their Floating Wonder sideshows. But in the spring of 1890 the brothers suddenly announced that they were closing down their booth and returning to the farm in Dexter. There were rumours that this had come about because Reynard had suddenly lost his strange power. Crowds of curious sightseers swarmed over the Beck farm, hoping to catch sight of Reynard, but he sternly refused to make any more public appearances and instead became a recluse. After publishing an account of his bizarre condition, Reynard begged for privacy. His last statement to the press in August 1890 was enigmatic: 'Once a man has flown in the air, he can never be quite the same man again'.

In September of that year, a rumour spread from Dexter and circulated around Middle America. It was said that the Floating Wonder had deliberately taken his belt off outdoors and had flown up into the sky to certain death by asphyxiation. The newshounds responded to the gossip by invading the Beck farm in droves, where they found a tearful Mrs Beck being comforted by her son Sam. They admitted that Reynard had been missing for three days and revealed that his weighted belt had been found in a field near the Tennessee border.

Reynard Beck was never seen again. Was the Flying Wonder a mammoth hoax perpetrated by the penurious Beck family? Or did the young farmer really levitate?

JAQUES CAZOTTE
The Prophet of Doom

The French 18th century writer Jaques Cazotte was a man of great imagination and foresight, and these talents are evident in his books. In *Le Diable Amourex* (1772), Cazotte tells the weird tale of a man who falls for a beautiful, voluptuous woman – who is really the Devil in disguise. Monsieur Cazotte also explored the sci-fi and fantasy genres long before the birth of Edgar Allan Poe. In his continuation of the *Arabian Nights* tales, the Frenchman wrote a series of astounding submarine adventures set in the Mediterranean. Some contemporaries credited Cazotte's literary talent to his infamous dabbling in the occult, which probably involved a ouija board and crystal-ball scrying.

Cazotte was also something of a prophet who scored more hits than misses, and because of his psychic ability, he was frequently invited to the salons of the rich and famous. At one such salon, on a pleasant summer evening in 1788, an assembly of notabilities settled down to a Parisian dinner party and talked of the approaching shadow of the Revolution, and the changes that were in store. Cazotte was invited to speak on the matter, and what he had to say caused a mixed reaction. Some laughed, but others shivered and protested when Cazotte told the gathering of writers, poets and courtiers that King Louis XVI, as well as several of the distinguished ladies sitting at the table, would be executed in the coming upheaval.

During the subsequent commotion, Cazotte stared at Nicholas Sebastian Chamfort, a writer and critic. Cazotte seemed to be focusing his powers of second sight. When the writer smiled at the seer's gaze, Cazotte started to speak in a low, disturbing voice. He told Chamfort,

"You will meet a long, suffering death after trying unsuccessfully to slash your wrists twenty-two times."

The writer shook his head and smiled, but seemed uneasy.

Cazotte then turned his attention to the Marquis de Condorcet, a prominent mathematician and philosopher whose progressive ideas helped to shape 19th century sociology. Cazotte told him, "You, sir, will die on the floor of a prison cell after taking poison to cheat the executioner."

"Nonsense!" protested a lady seated next to the Marquis, and she added indignantly, "How could someone as distinguished as the Marquis de Condorcet end up in a prison cell? Charlatan!"

The final prediction of Jaques Cazotte concerned Jean de la Harpe, a critic and bitter atheist. Cazotte told the non-believer that the Revolution would change him into a God-fearing Christian. Upon hearing this prophecy, one of the guests exploded with laughter and shouted, "All my fears are now gone, for if we have to wait until La Harpe becomes a Christian, we shall live forever!"

In 1789, the dreaded upheaval finally arrived in the form of the French Revolution, and with it came the abolition of the old order through mass executions on the guillotine. In the midst of this epic turmoil most men of learning either joined the revolutionaries, or fled the country.

Nicholas Chamfort decided to support the Revolution in its early stages, but later became sickened by the indiscriminate beheadings. In 1793, the year of the 'Reign of Terror', Chamfort was confronted by the Jacobin leaders and threatened with arrest. He knew he too would go to the guillotine sooner or later, so he cut his wrists to end it all – but committing suicide was more difficult than he had imagined. He slashed his wrists 22 times, and suffered an agonising death several days later, just as Cazotte had predicted.

As for the Marquis de Condorcet, he was actively involved in championing the revolutionary cause and was soon elected to represent the French capital in the Legislative Assembly. He went on to become its Secretary, and proposed a scheme for state education. He also agreed that the ex-King of France should be indefinitely suspended from his duties. The Marquis seemed to be a level-headed man of the people and went from strength to strength with the revolutionaries – until he voted against the execution of Louis XVI. The Marquis quickly fell out of favour with the rebels and when he also opposed the arrest of the Girondins, he was branded an enemy of the masses.

The Marquis went into hiding and became quite paranoid – convinced that the house he was hiding in was being watched. He went on the run for three exhausting days and under the cover of nightfall sought sanctuary in the village of Clamart. But somebody recognised him and he was taken to Bourg-la-Reine and imprisoned. The following morning he was found dead on the floor of the prison cell. He had poisoned himself to escape the guillotine – just as Cazotte had prophesied six years previously.

Like Chamfort and Condorcet, Jean de la Harpe, the final subject of Cazotte's prophecy, was also an advocate of the Revolution in its early days, but being a natural critic, he started to find faults with the new order and was soon classed as a dissenter and thrown into prison for five months. Within days of losing his freedom, the renowned atheist became a reformed man and ended up as an ardent supporter of Christianity, thus fulfilling Cazotte's prediction.

Jaques Cazotte's own fate is a sad one. In the superstitious age in which he lived, no rational attempt was made to investigate his strange powers of precognition, and so in 1792, he too became a suspected enemy of the people and was guillotined in Paris for being a Royalist. One wonders whether this man of incredible foresight actually saw his own fate years before in the Parisian salon.

ANDREW CROSSE
The Man Who was Frankenstein

According to scientists, life on earth began around four thousand million years ago when the world was a young, but forbidding planet. The turbulent atmosphere in those times was a mixture of steam, nitrogen, methane, ammonia, carbon and many other gases. But one gas was absent: oxygen. This gas is produced by plant life and did not exist in a free state before the arrival of life, so how exactly did life on earth begin? Well, established science holds that life came into being in an entirely accidental way. The lifeless matter floating about in the oceans of the early Earth supposedly consisted of various random molecules that collided with one another to form, by chance, a specific molecule which could reproduce copies of itself. But there are problems with this theory.

Protein chains – organic compounds containing the elements carbon, hydrogen, oxygen and nitrogen – consist of sub-units called amino acids, and there are 20 possibilities for each link in the protein chain. The French biophysicist Lecomte de Nony has calculated that if a new combination was tried every millionth of a second, it would take a period longer than the life of the earth to form the right type of protein chain! Nevertheless, scientists are adamant that life began in the world's primeval ocean-soup.

In 1952 it occurred to an American graduate student – Stanley Lloyd Miller – that an experiment to reproduce an environment conducive to life in primordial times could be set up in the laboratory. He put methane, ammonia, hydrogen and water in a flask and boiled the contents for days, occasionally discharging artificial lightning (via two electrodes) through the mixture to simulate the ultraviolet radiation of the sun. Miller observed that the mixture in the flask quickly darkened. After a week, he analysed the solution that had formed in the flask and found that, in addition to rudimentary substances lacking in nitrogen atoms, he had glycine and alanine, two simple amino acids. There were also minute traces of more complicated amino acids. Miller was surprised that the compounds had formed so quickly and in such large quantities.

The fact that Miller had created the building blocks of life in a laboratory, generated shockwaves which elated the scientific community and upset the religious authorities. But 115 years before Miller's experiment, a 53-year-old Englishman named Andrew Crosse had carried out a similar experiment. Crosse's experiment allegedly produced no mere amino acids, but the formation of a totally new type of insect.

Andrew Crosse was born into a wealthy family on 17 June 1784. He was a child prodigy who mastered Ancient Greek at the age of eight. When he was nine he was sent to Dr Seyer's School at Bristol, where he was captivated by science and around the age of twelve he became obsessed with the new science of electricity. Young Crosse was a notorious joker, and often wired up the metal doorknobs of the classroom doors to a huge accumulator, in order to give the teachers an electric shock whenever they entered the class.

Electricity was to become a lifetime obsession, and when the young science buff inherited the family estates and fortune upon the death of his mother in 1805, he used a substantial sum of his newly-acquired wealth to set up a well-equipped laboratory at Fyne Court, his family seat, where he was to perform a series of bizarre experiments.

The isolated country mansion in the Quantock Hills of Somerset soon gained an eerie reputation. The locals were sure Crosse was an evil wizard, because of the way he was able to capture the powers of lightning by conducting the bolts through a network of copper cables (over a mile in length) that radiated from the Fyne Court laboratory like a gigantic web. Whenever a storm raged over the Quantock Hills, the superstitious locals would watch the forks of lightning dancing about on the copper cables.

To the Somerset yokels, Squire Crosse had to be in league with the Devil, yet unknown to them, Crosse was tapping the huge voltages from the lightning flashes to power his electrical experiments. The scientist was intrigued by the various types of crystal that are formed when an electrical current is passed through certain mineral solutions. The results of this pioneering experimental work were written in a notebook, which includes an entry from 1837 recording a dramatic incident that has never been explained. The entry reads:

In the course of my endeavours to form artificial minerals by a long continued electric action on fluids holding in solution such substances as were necessary to my purpose, I had recourse to every variety of contrivance that I could think of; amongst others I constructed a wooden frame, which supported a Wedgewood funnel, within which rested a quart basin on a circular piece of mahogany. When this basin was filled with a fluid, a strip of flannel wetted with the same was suspended over the side of the basin and inside the funnel, which, acting as a syphon, conveyed the fluid out of the basin through the funnel in successive drops: these drops fell into a smaller funnel of glass placed beneath the other, and which contained a piece of somewhat porous red oxide from Vesuvius. This stone was kept constantly electrified.

On the fourteenth day from the commencement of this experiment, I observed through the lens a few small whitish excrescences, or nipples, projecting from about the middle of the electrified stone. On the eighteenth day these projections enlarged, and stuck out seven or eight filaments, each of them longer than the hemisphere on which they grew. On the twenty-sixth day these appearances assumed the form of a perfect insect, standing erect on a few bristles which formed its tail. On the twenty-eighth day these little creatures moved their legs ... After a few days they detached themselves from the stone, and moved about at pleasure.

Crosse was obviously amazed at the incredible outcome of his experiment, and he tried in vain to find a rational explanation that would account for the strange insect. He immediately repeated the experiment and again recorded the outcome in his notebook:

After many months' action and consequent formation of certain crystalline matters, I observed similar excrescences with those before described at the edge of the fluid in every one of the cylinders, except two which contained the carbonate of potassa and the metallic arsenic; and in due time the whitish appearances were developed into insects. In my first experiment I had made use of flannel, wood, and a volcanic stone. In the last, none of these substances were present.

But Crosse still could not accept what he was seeing. The existence of the new mites – or acari, as they are called, seemed to run contrary to the laws of biology. Determined to get to the bottom of the mite mystery, Crosse carried out the experiment yet again, and later wrote:

I had omitted to insert within the bulb of the retort a resting place for these acari (they are always destroyed if they fall back into the fluid from which they have emerged). It is strange that, in a solution eminently caustic and under an atmosphere of oxy-hydrogen gas, one single acarus should have made its appearance.

Crosse wrote a detailed report of his bizarre discovery and sent it to the Electrical Society in London. Although the report was sceptically received, WH Weeks, a respected experimenter, was chosen by the Electrical Society to repeat the Crosse experiment. Weeks was much more careful than Crosse at setting up the experiment. He thoroughly sterilised all of the lab equipment and worked under stringent quarantine-like conditions. News of the Crosse experiment broke as Weeks worked. A newspaper in the west of England published an account of it and soon the news agencies of Britain and the rest of Europe were running the story. Then the results of the Weeks experiment were announced: Weeks too had produced the strange insects.

The reclusive Crosse suddenly found himself in the eye of a hurricane of unwanted publicity. The mites he had created were named Acarus Crossii in his honour, and the creator-scientist was hailed as a genius by many of his colleagues. But the religious authorities and the ignorant hoi polloi were outraged by the 'blaspheming' Crosse, regarding him as a meddling devil who had set himself up as a rival of God. When Crosse returned to Fyne Court, the locals threw stones at him, killed his livestock and set fire to his crops. The local Reverend Philip Smith, who incited much of the trouble, even conducted a service of exorcism on the country estate!

On 6 July 1855, the controversial scientist died after suffering a paralytic seizure. His last words were: "The utmost extent of human knowledge is but comparative ignorance."

Even today, scientists cannot explain away the acari that were apparently created by Crosse, and what's more, no scientist is even willing to reproduce the fascinating 19th century experiment.

PRESTER JOHN
The Elusive Monarch Who Corresponded with Popes and Kings

In mediaeval times the European map of the world was surrounded on all sides by the mists of terra incognita and strange, seemingly endless seas. According to the map-makers of those times, the mysterious Atlantic Ocean was speckled with strange islands peopled by fairies and the dead, and terrifying gigantic serpents roamed the waters. The imaginative cartographers filled in the blank parts of the map representing unexplored regions with drawings of the exotic beasts of myth and fable: unicorns, dragons, griffins and one-eyed giants.

Factual knowledge of Africa and Asia was particularly scant – the Romans had known more of the 'Dark Continent' and the Far East centuries before in the days of Pliny; and Africa and the East remained as unknown to most mediaeval Europeans as the Moon is to the average man today. What hindered European expansion into the mysterious East was the vast Islamic empire which stretched from southern

Spain to the peripheries of China. The 'Christian' crusaders had, of course, gained some footholds in Syria and Palestine, but the 'menace' of Islam would not go away. So imagine how pleased the outnumbered Europeans in the Holy Land were when they heard tales of an unknown Christian monarch who ruled an immense kingdom near India (a generic term at the time for the unexplored lands beyond the River Tigris).

No one knows where the stories of the mysterious ruler originated, but the first definite record of an enigmatic priest-king known as 'Prester John' (his first name was derived from 'Presbyter' – Greek for 'priest') was made in 1145 when the French bishop Hugh de Gebal (now Lebanon) told the Pope of "a certain John, a king and a priest who dwells beyond Persia and Armenia in the uttermost East, and, with all his people, is a Christian. It is said that he is a lineal descendant of the Magi of whom mention is made in the gospel, and that ruling over the same peoples which they governed, he enjoys such great glory and wealth that he uses no sceptre, save one entirely of emerald. Inspired by the example of his forefathers who came to adore Christ in his manger, he had planned to go to the aid of Jerusalem, but was prevented from crossing the Tigris because the river was frozen."

This was sweet music to the ears of the Pope. For centuries there had been persistent rumours that Christian colonies existed in India, founded by the Apostle Thomas. Now the Pope was certain that India was christianised. The news of the good 'King of the Indies' flew across Europe. Prester John would be the ally who would help the Christian world to crush the Saracen hordes.

But nothing more was heard of the remote ruler until 1165, when three letters were sent to Pope Alexander III, the Byzantine Emperor Manuel, and the Holy Roman Emperor Frederick. The letters, written in Latin, read:

From Prester John, by the grace of God, most powerful king over all Christian kings. Let it be known to you that we have the highest crown on earth as well as gold, silver, precious stones, and strong fortresses, cities, towns, castles and boroughs. We have under our sway forty-two kings who are all mighty and good Christians.
Our land is divided into four parts, for there are so many Indias. In Greater India lies the body of the Apostle Saint Thomas, and this India is towards the east, for it is near the deserted Babylon and also near the tower called Babel.
Written in our holy palace in the land of Prester John.

The contents of this letter – which was quickly translated into all the principal European languages, and even Hebrew – surpassed all previous expectations of the priest-king's glory. Another grandiose letter from Prester John began:

We have been told that you would very much like to know about us and our country and our nation and our animals, and the nature of our country.

The writer of the royal epistle then goes on to paint an incredible picture of an incredible kingdom. In the sprawling country of the Four Indias, existed marvels such as the fabled race of beautiful blonde giantesses known as the Amazons, wild hares as large as sheep, the overgrown vestiges of the Garden of Eden, two bellicose races of cannibals known as Gog and Magog (imprisoned behind a chain of mountains in the far north of the country), a pepper forest infested by enormous snakes, strange cannabis-like plants that gave psychic powers to those who ate them, and the descendants of the ten lost tribes of Israel.

As for the way of life in the kingdom of Prester John, there were no thieves or adulterers, and poverty was unknown. The ruler had seven ravishing wives, but he only slept with them four nights a year. The court of the priest-king consisted of 30,000 people – and they enjoyed a royal banquet every day. At the right of Prester John, 12 archbishops sat, and at his left 23 bishops, including the Patriarch of St Thomas, the Bishop of Samarkand, and the Archbishop of Susa.

The claims of these letters will seem absurd to the modern-day reader, but to the Europeans of the 12th century, anything could exist in the Orient and the lands beyond, because no one had visited those realms to debunk the fabulous tales. So when the Greek and Roman emperors asked their scholars if the letters from Prester John were genuine, they judged them to be authentic. A Mecca for the adventurers of Europe was now sketched on the incomplete maps of the Orient and Asia: the Wondrous Kingdom of Prester John.

In 1177, Pope Alexander III became excited at the news brought back from travellers in the East about Prester John's desire to be instructed in the Catholic faith. The Pope's private physician, a Dr Philippus, had recently returned from an Eastern expedition with the news, and he also informed the Pope of Prester John's wish to build a church in Rome and his yearning to construct a fabulous altar in the Church of the Holy Sepulchre in Jerusalem.

The Pope was ecstatic, and he wrote a letter to the legendary monarch, which he gave to Dr Philippus to deliver. The physician set off on his mission – but was never heard from again. There were no further letters from Prester John, but in 1221, rumours of the priest-king began to circulate once again. It was said that a 'great Christian warlord was on the move in the East' – trouncing the Muslims with military manoeuvres reminiscent of the Romans. It was said that the holy warrior's path of conquest would soon bring him to Western Europe, where he would join up with his Christian brethren and launch a final attack to eradicate the Saracens from the face of the earth forever.

But this conquistador, according to the rumours, was not Prester John at all, for he had died by this time. The man who was to save Europe and Jerusalem from the adherents of Islam was Prester John's grandson, David.

No one took the rumours seriously, but a year later an army did arrive in Europe, and the leader of the hordes of strange-featured soldiers had a name that sounded like Prester John: his name was Genghis Khan – but he was anything but Christian. The Mongol armies of Genghis had recently plundered the citadel of Bukhara, where they slayed around 30,000 men and enslaved their wives and children. After the slaughter, the Great Khan climbed into the pulpit of the sacked city's mosque and delivered his chilling sermon:

"Oh people! Know that you have committed great sins! If you ask me what proof I have for these words, I say it is because I am the punishment of God! If you had not committed great sins, God would not have sent a punishment like me upon you!"

The Mongolian warrior who today ranks in notoriety with Alexander the Great, Napoleon and Hitler, was backed by an army of a size that had not been witnessed in Europe since the days of the Roman invasions. A Persian civil servant of the time wrote of the Mongol swarm:

The troops of the Great Khan were more numerous than ants or locusts, being in their multitude beyond estimation or computation. Detachment after detachment arrived, each like a billowing sea.

Russia, Poland and Hungary were ravaged by the Tartar armies, but fortunately, Genghis Khan had to return to Asia to settle a squabble in the Mongolian royal dynasty, and his forces left Europe badly bruised, but unbeaten. The empire of Khan, which stretched from the Pacific to the Danube, made the old Islamic threat now seem microscopic in comparison. Fears of a new Mongol menace proved to be unfounded. The Mongol empire made it clear that it had no intention of absorbing the West, and trade routes, policed by the Tartar horsemen, soon opened up, providing Europeans with safe highways to the lands of the beckoning East. At last, the search for Prester John could soon begin in earnest.

As the Mongols were pagans, it was hoped in the West that they could be converted to Christianity and then join in the Holy War against the Muslims. So the first travellers who ventured into Asia were monks and friars, such as John of Plano Carpini and William of Ruysbruck. These holy men managed to convert some of the

Tartars and returned to give encouraging news of an Asia inhabited by a largely peaceful population. Many European merchants were captivated by the promising tales of Asia and Cathay and hit the roads to the East, hoping to buy spices, furs, precious stones, and perhaps to form alliances with the powerful khans of Mongolia. The best known of these travellers was a Venetian by the name of Marco Polo, who first visited Peking in 1275.

Polo actually claimed to have located the long-sought kingdom of Prester John. According to Polo, Prester John's kingdom was Tenduk, a large domain in the north of Mongolia, and he was murdered by his own vassal – Genghis Khan. At the time of Polo's visit to Tenduk, the ruler was a Christian God-fearing man who still held the title of Prester John. What's more, a majority of the inhabitants of Tenduk were also Christian.

Of all the travellers to the East, Marco Polo was the least likely to invent fanciful tales, so did he find the Kingdom of Prester John? No one is sure, even today. Many historians believe that the kingdom was probably simply an embroidered description of the Abyssinian Church. Shortly after the death of Christ, the African Church was founded in Abyssinia (now known as Ethiopia), a region ringed by almost impenetrable mountains, and until the 16th century, this remote outpost of the Christian faith survived behind the Islamic barrier of Egypt. The Abyssinian church was never attacked by the Muslims because it was said that when the prophet Mohammed announced his mission to all the kings of the world, it was only the ruler of Abyssinia who was courteous enough to send a punctilious reply.

The holy Abyssinian king ruled over a vast territory that certainly bears some resemblance to the strange land of Prester John. Abyssinia was exceedingly rich in mineral resources, and on the outskirts of the country there lived a tribe of pygmies and an exceptionally tall race, both now extinct. The Abyssinian monarch was said to be a direct descendant of King Solomon, a claim that was upheld by Haile Selassie, the 20th century Emperor of Ethiopia.

So, is that it? Was Prester John just an inflated yarn based on an Ethiopian king? Not quite. When the Ambassador of Abyssinia arrived in Rome in 1441, he strenuously denied that his sovereign was named 'John'.

"No! His true and only name is Zareiacob, meaning 'Descendant of the prophet Jacob'," he insisted.

Our file on Prester John, then, must remain open.

THE MAN IN THE IRON MASK
The Prisoner Who Could Not Show His Face

In the sixtieth year of King Louis XIV's reign, an enigmatic individual known as the 'ancient prisoner', died in the Bastille. The reason for the man's 34-year incarceration was never divulged, but today, thanks to the romantic novelist Alexandre Dumas and his book *The Man in the Iron Mask*, we all know the bizarre aspects of his imprisonment. Dumas popularised the notion that the Bastille's most famous prisoner was either the Sun King himself or his twin brother, and that the prisoner wore an iron mask, but the real facts concerning the masked prisoner are much more mysterious. All that is known for certain is that in July 1669, a man was arrested in Dunkirk (which was then in English hands); whether this man was entering or leaving the country has never been established. He was taken to the prison fortress at Pignerol (near Turin) in Piedmont, north-west Italy. Monsieur Saint Mars, the governor of the prison, had received a letter from the French Minister of War, the Marquis de Louvois, telling him to take extraordinary security precautions with the prisoner:

The king has commanded that I am to have the man [the prisoner] named Eustache Dauger sent to Pignerol. It is of the most importance to His service that he should be most securely guarded and that he should in no way give information about himself nor send letters to anyone at all. I am informing you of this in advance so that you can have a cell prepared in which you will place him securely, taking care that the windows of the place in which he is put do not give on to any place that can be approached by anyone, and that there are double doors to be shut, for your guards must not hear anything. You must yourself take to him, once a day, the day's necessities and you must never listen, under any pretext whatever, to what he may want to reveal to you, always threatening to kill him if he ever opens his mouth to speak of anything but his day-to-day needs.

Shortly after Dauger arrived at Pignerol, the prison governor wrote back to the Marquis de Louvois, confirming the prisoner's arrival:

Monsieur de Vauroy [the military governor of Dunkirk] has handed over to me the man named Eustache d'Auger [sic]. As soon as I had put him in a very secure place, while waiting for the cell I am having prepared for him to be completed, I told him in the presence of Monsieur de Vauroy that if he should speak to me or anyone else of anything other than his day-today needs, I would run him through with my sword. On my life, I shall not fail to observe, very punctiliously, your commands.

This obviously suggests that Dauger was no ordinary prisoner, and that he had information that posed some sort of dire threat to the security of the realm. In March 1698, Saint-Mars was given the post of governor at the Bastille and Dauger was transferred with him to Paris, this time forced to wear a black velvet mask with metal clasps.

The arrival of the masked prisoner naturally made everyone in the Bastille curious. The gossipers at the prison had a field day. Some said that the strange prisoner was the illegitimate offspring of the Queen Mother and her Chief Minister, Cardinal Mazarin, while others believed that the prisoner was the real Louis XIV and that the king of France was an illegitimate son. Voltaire, one of the greatest intellects of his age (and the man who invented the myth of the 'iron' mask), proposed that the prisoner in the mask was an illegitimate half-brother of Louis XIV, the result of an act of infidelity by the Queen of Louis XIII.

There was no shortage of theories, but the only person who ever saw the face of the prisoner was Saint-Mars, and he never revealed what he knew. A doctor who once examined the man in the mask never actually got to see his face; he inspected only the man's tongue and his naked body, noting that the prisoner had dark skin, and was 'admirably made'. He also said that the enigmatic captive had an 'interesting voice', but never elaborated further on this curious remark.

In 1703, the man in the mask died at the Bastille. All the furniture and personal belongings in his cell were burned, and the surfaces of the cell's walls scraped and whitewashed in case the prisoner had engraved a message. Even the tiles on the floor were replaced. The faceless 'ancient prisoner' who had lived his prison life in such anonymity was buried in an unmarked grave. The name on his burial certificate names him Marchioly, which only deepens the mystery surrounding his identity.

The most important clue to his identity must lie in the mask. Why was it so important for his face to remain concealed for so long? Did he bear a striking resemblance to some prominent person in France? The fact that a special governor was appointed to the masked prisoner for all of his life means he must have been someone of note. Why wasn't he simply executed after his arrest at Dunkirk? Was he allowed to live – because he meant too much to someone in power? Several historical revisionists have come to the conclusion that Voltaire may have hit the nail on the head when he suggested that the prisoner was the half-brother of Louis XIV.

Another unusual theory that has been put forward in recent years is that the prisoner was the real father of Louis XIV. It is known that for 13 of their 22 years of marriage, Louis XIII and his queen, Anne of Austria, had no children, because the king was impotent. Cardinal Richelieu – who was at the time the effective ruler of France – knew it was in the interests of the monarch to produce an heir (who could also become the puppet king of the Richelieu faction). The couple had separated, but Richelieu used his diplomatic skills to get them back together for a reconciliation, and the result of this rapprochement was the birth of a boy in 1638.

The news of the birth shocked the French nation, as it was widely known that the royal couple detested one another, and many thought it strange that the king and Queen – who had never had a child before – were suddenly able to produce an heir. It has been suggested that the unprincipled Richelieu persuaded the Queen to have sexual intercourse with a young nobleman in order to produce an heir to the throne. This nobleman would probably have been one of the bastard sons of the promiscuous Henry of Navarre – all half-brothers of King Louis XIII – which would have meant that the Queen's lover had royal Bourbon blood in his veins. This theory would certainly explain why Louis XIV was so unlike his royal 'father'. Perhaps the masked prisoner had to have his face concealed because of the tell-tale resemblance he bore to his son. This would also explain why the 'Sun King' never had the most famous prisoner of the Bastille secretly murdered; that would have been patricide.

POPE JOAN
The Strange Tale of the Pope Who Gave Birth

In this day and age of sexual equality, the notion of a woman disguising herself as a man to gain entry into a male-dominated career seems absurd and demeaning, but there have been numerous cases throughout history of females dressing up as men to further themselves.

One such example was an upwardly-mobile female transvestite named Dr James Barry, a dashing, handsome army surgeon who served in the West Indies, South Africa and India. In 1808, at the age of 16, he was accepted as a medical student at Edinburgh University, and ended up as a prominent surgeon. When he died at the age of 73 on 25 July 1865, many mourned the popular old man's passing. Then came the startling revelation at his post-mortem examination: Dr Barry was in fact a woman.

He had breasts and a vagina. Furthermore, the post-mortem revealed that 'Mr Barry' had given birth to a child in her youth, but what became of her offspring is a secret that the unidentified woman took with her to the grave.

Another bizarre case of a woman masquerading as a man is said to have taken place around 864 AD in Rome. The first mention of this incredible and heretical tale is to be found in an obscure manuscript in the Vatican Library at Rome. In a yellow, time-worn tome that is now hidden from the light of day, a 9th century Roman scribe named Anastasius Bibliothecarius tells the story of a woman who, after passing herself off as a man, was elected Pope! The scribe's account is today classified by the Vatican as a blasphemous, apocryphal fable, but other writers since Bibliothecarius have also recorded more detailed accounts of 'Pope Joan' – as she was allegedly known. In the 11th century, Martinus Scotus, a monk from the Abbey of St Martin of Cologne in Germany, wrote: 'In AD 854, Lotharii 14, Joanna, a woman, succeeded Leo, and reigned two years, five months, and four days.'

A 12th century scribe known as Sigebert de Gemlours, also wrote of the controversial event:

> It is reported that this John was a female, and that she conceived a child by one of her servants. The Pope, becoming pregnant, gave birth to a child, whereof some do not number her among the Pontiffs.

The 13th century scribe Stephen of Bourbon also alludes to the existence of Pope Joan in his religious work, *De Septem Donis Spiritu Sancti* (Of the Seven Gifts of the Holy Spirit) but he is very reticent about the exact details of the story. The only reliable and detailed account of the Pope Joan episode is contained in the pages of *Chronicron Pontificum et Imperatum* (The Chronicle of the Popes and Emperors), written by the 13th century annalist, Martin of Troppau. He writes:

> After Leo IV, John Anglus, a native of Metz, reigned two years, five months and four days. And the pontificate was vacant for a month. He died in Rome. He is related to have been a female, and when a girl, to have accompanied her sweetheart in male costume to Athens; there she advanced in various sciences and none could be found to equal her. So, after having studied for three years in Rome, she had great masters for her pupils and hearers. And when there arose a high opinion in the city of her virtue and knowledge, she was unanimously elected Pope. But during her papacy she became in the family way by a familiar. Not knowing the time of the birth, as she was on her way from St Peter's to Lateran, she had a painful delivery, between the Coliseum and St Clement's Church, in the street. Having died after, it is said she was buried on the spot.

And where is this spot where Joan was irreverently interred? It is said to have been indicated by a large stone slab, inscribed with a very concise summary of the blasphemous woman who laid beneath it. But because the stone was becoming an embarrassment to the Church, Pope St Pius V (1566-72) had it removed and broken up. After the Pope Joan Scandal, all papal candidates were forced to undergo a brief physical examination to prove their gender.

In 1557, a century after the advent of the movable type which had made the mass-production of books possible, the Catholic Church drew up a list of censored writers and their books. One of the first scribes to appear on the list of prohibited books, or the 'Index Librorum Prohibitorum' as it was officially known, was Giovanni Boccaccio, an Italian writer. His book of one hundred licentious stories, *The Lives of the Decameron*, which took ten years to write, happened to mention the story of Pope Joan, and was immediately placed on the Index. Boccaccio later reissued a sanitised version of his epic tome, minus all the sinning monks and nuns; he was subsequently forgiven and the ban on his book was lifted. But with the Reformation in full swing, the Protestant pamphleteers saw the Pope Joan story as excellent propaganda, and error-strewn printed accounts and word-of-mouth tales of the 'Popess' were soon circulating throughout Europe, and with each retelling of the story, the details became more sordid.

In England, it was said that Joan's first lover had been a Benedictine monk, her second paramour a cardinal, and that she had even ended up copulating with Lucifer himself! Because of the bitter anti-Catholicism that swept western Europe, the story of Pope Joan was distorted until it bore no resemblance to the original account, and as the Vatican is still withholding most of the intriguing references about the incident in its subterranean library, we simply don't have the necessary information which would enable us to determine if the female Pope ever existed.

RICHARD BINGHAM
The Case of the Vanishing Peer

At 9.45 on the evening of Thursday 7 November 1974, a petite brunette in a bloodstained nightdress burst into the bar of the Plumbers Arms public house in London's exclusive Belgravia district. To a handful of startled drinkers, the woman shouted: "Help me! Help me! I've just escaped from being murdered! My children! He's in the house! He's just murdered my nanny!"

The woman, who had sustained seven bloody head wounds, was 37-year-old Lady Lucan, wife of Richard Bingham, Lord Lucan, and the murderer she spoke of was her estranged husband.

Arthur Whitehouse, the barman of the Plumbers Arms, dialled 999 while his wife treated Lady Lucan's head injuries until an ambulance arrived. Ten minutes later a police van pulled up outside the pub. After being quizzed by detectives, Lady Lucan was taken to the casualty ward at St George's Hospital, Hyde Park Corner.

Meanwhile, Sergeant Baker and Police Constable Beddick arrived at the alleged scene of the crime – Lady Lucan's terraced house at Number 46 Belgrave Street, a mere stone's throw from Buckingham Palace. The two policemen saw that the house was in darkness and tried to peer into the living room of the raised ground floor, but net curtains prevented them from seeing anything. They descended the outside stairs which led to the basement, and through a window saw the faint glow of a red lamp on an electric kettle beyond the venetian blinds. The officers then returned to the front door of the house and finding it locked, decided to force it open.

Inside, they found that the hall light wasn't working. Thinking the murderer could still be lurking in the dark hall, Sergeant Baker told PC Beddick to fetch a torch from the patrol car. Baker produced a small pocket torch and went into the house. By the faint light of his torch Sergeant Baker noticed streaks of wet blood on the wallpaper at the end of the hall.

Beddick re-entered the house with a powerful torch and rejoined the Sergeant. Together, they slowly descended the stairs to the basement, following the trail of blood. At the foot of the stairs was a large pool of blood, within which the faint outlines of a number of footprints could be discerned. The basement was quickly checked, but finding no intruder present, the two policemen proceeded to search the rest of the six-story house.

Upon entering a bedroom on the second floor, they found a bloodstained towel draped across a pillow. The two policemen then heard sounds emanating from the floor above. They went upstairs and discovered that the sounds were coming from a colour television set that had been left on in the nursery. For some inexplicable reason, the volume control had been fully turned up.

On the top floor, Baker and Beddick found Lady Lucan's children. Two of them were sleeping soundly, but the third, ten-year-old Frances, was wide-awake and standing by her bed. "Where are Mummy and Sandra?" she asked. The Sandra she referred to was 29-year-old Sandra Rivett, the nanny of Lady Lucan's children.

As soon as the children had been put safely in the care of a summoned police officer, Baker and Beddick resumed their inspection of the basement. They discovered a canvas United States mail bag near the foot of the basement steps next to the door of the kitchen. An arm was protruding from it. Inside the mail bag was the body of the nanny, Mrs Rivett. She had been bludgeoned to death. The body was still warm, but no pulse was present. Shortly afterwards, detectives found the murder weapon in the ante room off the hall. It was a nine-inch-long piece of lead piping, bound in surgical tape.

Detectives made routine inquiries and started piecing together events. Later that eventful night, Detective Sergeant Graham Forsyth called at Lucan's flat at 72a Elizabeth Street. Lucan wasn't there. At 10.45pm, Lucan telephoned his 75-year-old mother, the Dowager Countess of Lucan. He told her that there had been a 'terrible catastrophe at Number 46' and that his wife and her nanny had been badly hurt. Lucan went on to tell his mother how he had been driving past his wife's house when he saw a fight in progress through the blinds of the basement window. He went in and saw 'something terrible in the basement'. "I couldn't bring myself to look," he explained. Lucan's mother asked her son where he was going. Before he hung up, Lucan replied, "I don't know."

In his dark blue Ford Corsair, Lucan travelled 42 miles south to the village of Uckfield in Sussex. At 11.30pm he called at the home of Susan Maxwell-Scott, a long-standing friend. When she answered the door, the shocked and dishevelled-looking peer asked Susan if her husband Ian (another close associate of Lucan) was around. Mrs Maxwell-Scott said he wasn't at home, and asked Lucan what was wrong. Lucan said, "I have been through a nightmarish experience. It's so incredible, I don't think you or anyone else could possibly believe it."

Lucan then reiterated the same story he had told his mother. Mrs Maxwell-Scott urged Lucan to visit the police with her first thing in the morning, but Lucan said that was out of the question. At 1.15am he drove off into the night, never to be seen again. Later that morning, around eight o'clock, his abandoned car was found parked outside a house in the south coast port of Newhaven. Inside the vehicle, on the front seats, dashboard and steering wheel, were smears of dried blood. In the boot, the police found a second length of lead piping wrapped in sticking plaster.

Detectives took a statement from Lady Lucan in hospital. According to her version of events, shortly before nine o'clock on the night of the murder, she and Sandra Rivett had been watching television with the three children in the nursery on the third floor. After putting the two younger children to bed, Mrs Rivett went downstairs to the basement kitchen to make a cup of tea. When she had failed to return after 20 minutes, Lady Lucan became suspicious and went down to see what was wrong. As she reached the dark hallway, she called out the nanny's name, but received no reply.

Lady Lucan walked down the steps to the basement, when suddenly, Lord Lucan leaned over the banister and started beating her over the head with a length of lead pipe. He landed seven blows to her skull, but incredibly Lady Lucan remained conscious and fought her attacker. Her husband thrust his gloved hand down her throat and attempted to throttle her. Lady Lucan then grabbed his testicles and squeezed them as hard as she could. This did the trick and Lucan quickly let go of her.

The exhausted couple then decided to talk things over. Lucan helped his wife upstairs, then went to the bathroom to fetch a towel. Lady Lucan took the opportunity to flee from the house, heading straight for the Plumbers Arms, a mere 30 yards away.

Scotland Yard launched a nationwide manhunt, and Interpol later joined in the search. Unconfirmed sightings of the aristocratic fugitive started coming in from places as remote as New Delhi and Paraguay, but subsequent investigations established that most of the sightings were cases of mistaken identity.

A month after the murder, the suspicions of the Australian police were aroused when a distinguished-looking Englishman turned up in Melbourne. He was promptly arrested and grilled. It turned out not to be Lucan, but the former Labour government minister John Stonehouse, wanted by police in Britain after faking his suicide in Florida in order to escape from business problems.

Because Lucan had relatives in South Africa, many believed that the various sightings of the peer in Johannesburg were probably genuine. Detective Chief Superintendent Roy Ranson, who was assigned to the Lucan case from day one, firmly believes that Richard Bingham is hiding out in South Africa.

In 1994, shortly after his retirement, Ranson published *Looking For Lucan*, an intriguing account of his ongoing search for the peer. The book is laced with controversial hints and allegations. Ranson draws attention to some startling and previously-unknown facts and links which add a new dimension to the renowned murder case, such as Lucan's frequent use of a private plane, and his friendship with racing driver Graham Hill – a seasoned pilot who died in 1976 when his twin-engined Piper Aztec crashed near his home at Elstree.

Did Hill fly Lucan out of Britain? According to Ranson, Hill regularly flew all over Europe (often with a total disregard for European aviation laws) and had once transported Lucan's Mercedes car from Britain to the peer's Estoril villa in Portugal – but Ranson admits that we will probably never know if Hill performed an even greater and controversial favour for Bingham in November 1974.

Channel Four Television commissioned a documentary team to follow the retired Ranson in his quest for the shadowy aristocrat, but despite a number of interviews with people who had allegedly encountered Lucan, the programme ended on a disappointingly inconclusive note.

The bookmakers, Ladbroke's, once offered 1000-1 odds against Lucan ever being found. But the odds were later withdrawn. Did Lucan commit suicide, or is he still hiding from justice? If the latter is true, he is presumably being sheltered, but by whom?

VALENTINE GREATRAKES
The Irish Healer They Called 'The Stroker'

Being born on 14 February 1629, it was decided by his parents that their baby boy would be called Valentine, but none of the Irish Greatrakes family could have suspected that the babe would one day become a famous and controversial healer, whose fame would travel across Europe.

The young Valentine Greatrakes was as normal as any other child, and he exhibited no out-of-the-ordinary talents in the early stages of his life in Affane, County Waterford, where he was brought up in the Protestant tradition of Ireland.

At the age of 20, Greatrakes began his seven-year military career as an officer in the Parliamentary army during the English Civil War. He was a loyal cavalry lieutenant for Cromwell, and when he was discharged in 1656, he was rewarded by the Lord Protector with a number of high-powered appointments, including that of Justice of the Peace. With the Restoration of 1660, the reinstatement of the English monarchy under Charles II – Greatrakes lost his civil appointments, but he was later made High Sheriff of Waterford.

In 1663, at the age of 34, Greatrakes had a series of strange recurrent dreams in which he received the gift of healing from a God-like being. He told his wife about the strange repetitive dream, and she told him not to worry about it, but shortly afterwards he experienced, while awake this time, what he described as 'an impulse, or strange persuasion to heal'. Again, Valentine told his wife about 'preternatural forces' that were inwardly urging him to cure people. She suggested he should try to put his thoughts into practice, by attempting to heal the poor disfigured people to whose medical treatment she charitably contributed. Greatrakes followed his wife's suggestion, and later wrote of the first unfortunate individual he encountered:

There was one at hand that had the Evil grievously in the eyes, throat and cheeks, whereupon I laid my hands upon the places affected, and prayed to God for Jesus's sake to heal him. In a few days afterwards, the father brought the son, with the eye so much changed that it was almost quite whole, and to be brief (to God's glory I speak it) within a month he was perfectly healed and so continues.

Being a rather squeamish man, Greatrakes felt quite nauseous at the sight of the victims of scrofula – a tuberculosis of the lymphatic glands that was also known as 'king's evil' after Edward the Confessor (c 1042-66), who is recorded to have healed victims by 'royal touch'. In England, Scotland and France, it had long been thought that the touch of a royal hand was a sure remedy for scrofula and similar disfiguring diseases.

Scarcely was Charles I on the throne when he too began to demonstrate his curative powers, and scores of scrofulous people flocked from far and near to benefit from his touch. When he became Lord Protector, even Oliver Cromwell attempted to continue the tradition of the royal touch, but failed.

Greatrakes treated another victim of Scrofula, a woman named Margaret MacShane, who had been unsuccessfully treated by a certain Dr Anthony, a well-known physician of the day. Greatrakes visited the woman and later described how his healing hands:

... suppurated the nodes and drew and healed the sores which formerly I could not have endured the sight of, nor touched, nor smelt without vomiting, so great an aversion had I naturally to all wounds and sores.

Amazingly, Margaret MacShane made a miraculous recovery over a period of six weeks, and was completely cured. Scrofula was just one of a host of diseases rife in the 17th century. Greatrakes decided to test his healing powers on a victim of the ague, a feverish, convulsive condition that was as widespread as scrofula. Again he met with success, and by 1665 – the year in which the Great (bubonic) Plague killed 68,000 Londoners – the news of Greatrakes's healing ability had spread like wildfire. The Irishman was soon healing the sick from six in the morning till six in the evening, three days a week, and so many people visited his home, he had to build out-houses to accommodate them.

But Greatrakes's fame also reached the ears of the ecclesiastical authorities, and the 'Irish Mesmerist' – as some called him – was summoned by the Dean of Lismore to appear before a bishop's court. The result of this was that Greatrakes was forbidden to practise, but he angrily ignored the injunction, and such was his popularity, and his social standing, that the religious authorities were powerless to take further action against him.

The Leonardo da Vinci of his day, a brilliant Irish physicist named Robert Boyle, John Evelyn, the diarist and founder of the Royal Society, the poet Andrew Marvell, and the journalist Roger L'Estrange all paid a visit to Valentine Greatrakes when he visited plague-stricken London, and the latter was surprised to learn first-hand that the famous healer was not taking money for his cures. The journalist also interviewed a woman who had been cured of deafness, blindness, cancer, sciatica, and palsy. By this time, Greatrakes had earned the nickname of 'The Stroker' because of the way he moved his hands with a stroking motion above the affected part of the patient's body without actually touching them. Robert Boyle subjected the Stroker to a thorough investigation and declared him to be a genuine healer, although John Evelyn believed that Greatrakes's health-restoring talents were only effective against certain ailments. The diarist wrote:

To my observation, the cures he commonly pretended to were most effectively on tumours, aches, rheumatisms and other wandering distempers; but did not extend to fevers, agues, pleurisies, etc, where the habit is vitiated. However, I say the history is by no means to be slighted.

Andrew Marvell was greatly impressed by the Stroker's successful treatment of plague victims, and many of London's prominent academics and physicians also spoke in favour of Greatrakes.

In 1683, Valentine Greatrakes died at the age of 54. No one has ever given an adequate explanation for the Irishman's gift. It is said that as Greatrakes got older, the strange faculty began to fade, but those close to him insisted that his healing power had not diminished; he had merely withdrawn from public view because certain dogmatic clergymen, fearing obsolescence, had hounded him with baseless accusations of witchcraft.

ALICE
The Girl from the Looking-Glass

Thanks to the work of the German physicist Albert Einstein (1879-1955), we now know that the space around us is not the fixed, invariant, absolute thing it was once regarded as being. In his *General Theory of Relativity* (1915), Einstein predicted that an object with a sufficiently strong gravitational field would be able to curve a beam of light in its vicinity. Many scientists scoffed at this claim, but numerous tests have proved him correct.

The first test, in 1919, took place during a total eclipse of the Sun which was visible from the Portuguese-owned island of Principe off West Africa. British astronomers who had gathered on the island to witness the eclipse saw that the stars nearest to the edge of the eclipsed Sun were in positions that did not tally with their usual co-ordinates, because the Sun's massive gravitational field was warping the beams of starlight, thus presenting a distorted image of the stars to observers on Earth.

Then, in 1962, Professor John A Wheeler of Princeton, the co-inventor of the H-bomb, and physicist Robert W Fuller, delivered a paper entitled, *Causality and Multiply-Connected Space-Time*, outlining their theory of 'superspace' – a bizarre form of space that exists 'next door' to our space. Fuller and Wheeler's paper is rather too abstruse to go into here, but in a nutshell, they say that the ten field equations of the General Theory of Relativity suggest that there is an immense region of a peculiar type of space that permeates every part of the known universe. Entrances and exits to and from this superspace exist everywhere, but are incredibly hard to find. Wheeler surmises that these portals in superspace may one day be used as an instantaneous route to the stars and other dimensions. Perhaps one of Wheeler's illusive portals can explain the following story.

One uncomfortable, sticky summer night in July 1963, ten-year-old Kathy Hodson, a pretty little girl with long blonde hair and sky-blue eyes, was having trouble getting to sleep. Her bedroom on the top floor of the three story house overlooked Hampstead Heath, in North London. Kathy had been playing on the Heath all day but she wasn't tired. She turned in her bed, punched her pillow, then settled down, glancing about the room. She looked at the large mirror hanging on the wall. It measured three feet in length and two feet in width, and an ornate frame of golden leaves ran around it. Kathy was staring at the reflection of the drawn bedroom curtains in the mirror, when something happened which would haunt the girl for the rest of her life. A face appeared in the mirror – the face of a blonde-haired girl who looked the same age as Kathy.

Kathy Hodson blinked at the other girl, and a cold shiver ran up her spine. Kathy closed her eyes for a while, gulped, then looked at the mirror again to see that the girl was still there, only now she was smiling. The smile had a reassuring effect on Kathy, but when the apparition faded away, her heart sank. She got out of bed and bravely inspected the mirror, staring at her own reflection and wondering who the strange visitor had been. She had a feeling that the girl in the looking-glass had wanted to be friends with her – but where was she from and where had she gone to?

Kathy went back to bed and lay awake until the early hours of the morning, waiting for the girl to reappear, but she never did, and she finally fell asleep.

About a month later, the same face again appeared in Kathy's bedroom mirror. This time the girl seemed to be giggling, but made no sound. As soon as the excited Kathy jumped from her bed to greet the girl, much to her annoyance the vision disappeared. Around this time, Kathy gave her spectral friend a name: she decided to call her Alice, after the heroine in Lewis Carroll's fantasy tales. After the second appearance, Kathy's mother was baffled by her daughter's over-enthusiasm to get to bed. Kathy tried to tell her mother what she had seen, but the words died on her lips because she just knew no one would believe her.

At the beginning of December that year, Kathy was having a hot bath. She was thinking of Christmas, which was a fortnight away, and then her thoughts turned to her best friend, Gracie Sennet, who had been tucked up in bed for a couple of days because of a bad cold. Kathy hoped Gracie would be well in time for Christmas.

After her bath, Kathy was put to bed, and within a few minutes was fast asleep, but at midnight, as the old grandfather clock began to strike twelve, Kathy awoke and heard a faint voice calling her name. She realised it was coming from the mirror on the wall. She sat up in bed and stared at the looking-glass, and to her astonishment, she saw an uncanny circle of green light flickering on it. 'Alice' appeared, and this time something truly incredible happened: the girl in the looking-glass stepped out of the mirror, jumped down onto the floor and approached Kathy. She wore a quaint, out-dated white nightdress, but this time Alice was not smiling: she looked quite sombre.

Kathy was not in the least bit frightened by the visitation, because she wanted Alice to accompany her into her parents' bedroom so that they could see her incredible friend. Kathy threw back the covers and left her bed to embrace Alice, but the girl reacted by backing away towards the mirror.

"Oh, please don't go!" Kathy pleaded.

Alice then seemed to lose solidity and slid back into the mirror, looking right at Kathy as she did so.

"Don't go, Alice. I won't hurt you," said Kathy, "Please come and play with me."

An aura of pale green light shone around the looking-glass girl, and as Kathy approached the mirror, she said in a softly-spoken voice,

"No! Don't come any closer. You mustn't."

"Why not?" asked Kathy, stopping in her tracks.

"I have not called to play. There is another reason," replied Alice.

Kathy did not understand what Alice meant. She watched, feeling perplexed as the girl in the mirror raised her hand and pointed to the window.

"Your friend Gracie is very ill," Alice said, mournfully. "You must help her. She didn't listen to what her mother told her. She has taken too many of the pills which the doctor left for her chill. If you don't help her quickly, she will die."

Before Kathy could ask Alice how she knew this, the figure in the mirror vanished and Kathy was suddenly alone again, looking at her own reflection. She wondered what she should do. If she told her mother about Alice, she'd just say the incident had been some sort of nightmare. But Gracie's life depended on her doing something, so Kathy reluctantly left her bedroom, walked along the landing, and after hesitating for a moment, opened the door of her parents' bedroom and woke her mother.

"What is it, Kathy?" Mrs Hodson asked.

Kathy told her mother about Alice and her warning, but Mrs Hodson responded to the account by simply embracing her daughter.

"You were dreaming, darling. Gracie is being well looked after. She'll be fine, don't worry. You've had a bad dream, that's all," she assured her.

"But it wasn't a dream. It wasn't," persisted Kathy, trying to make her mother understand.

"Go back to bed, dear," yawned her mother. "You can go over to see Gracie in the morning. You'll see, she's fine."

Mrs Hodson patted her concerned-looking daughter on the head and went back to sleep.

After waiting a moment, Kathy sneaked downstairs to the kitchen. She picked up the phone and dialled Gracie's number which she knew off by heart. The girl listened to the ringing tone. It seemed to go on forever, but was suddenly interrupted by a click and a woman's voice. It was Gracie's mother.

"Hello, Mrs Sennet?" said Kathy, self-consciously.

"Is that you, Kathy?" asked Mrs Sennet, surprised at such a late call from her daughter's friend.

"Yes, er ..." Kathy muttered.

"What on earth are you doing ringing up at this time of night? You should be in bed? Is your mother there?" Mrs Sennet asked.

"Oh, Mrs Sennet, I have to know if Gracie is well. You see, something strange has happened," said Kathy, and she explained in detail what had driven her to make the nightcall.

"What a lot of nonsense, Kathy. You must have been dreaming. Of course Gracie is alright. The doctor came today and gave her some pills to help her get a good night's sleep, and that's what you need my girl. Now hurry back to bed before your mother catches you!"

"But Mrs Sennet ..." Kathy persisted, trying to get a word in.

"Goodnight!" Mrs Sennet said firmly, and slammed her phone down.

Kathy hung up the phone and went upstairs to her bedroom, but she was unable to fall asleep because she was so worried. She tossed and turned for over an hour, unable to settle until she could be sure that Gracie was alright, so, once more, she woke her mother. Mrs Hodson was a little cross to say the least! To make matters worse, Kathy told her mum that she had also warned Mrs Sennet on the phone.

"You silly little girl! As if that poor woman hasn't got enough on her mind!" Mrs Hodson bawled, and she got out of bed and went downstairs to the phone to apologise to Mrs Sennet.

Kathy felt as if she was going to burst into tears, the way she always felt when her mother shouted at her. She followed her mother downstairs, and started to sniffle.

Mrs Hodson phoned Mrs Sennet and glared at Kathy as she started to apologise for her daughter's late-night call, but soon her mother stopped speaking and her jaw dropped. Kathy listened to the faint, tinny, but audible sound of Mrs Sennet's reply.

"Oh, there's no need to apologise. In fact, it's a blessing she did call. You see, it made me go and check on Gracie, just in case. Lucky I did, Gracie had taken the whole bottle of pills. She thought if one pill would make her better, all of them would get her well in time for Christmas. I called the doctor and the poor little thing's had her stomach pumped. Thank goodness, the doctor says she'll be alright. I don't know how on earth Kathy knew what she'd done, but she saved Gracie's life."

When Mrs Hodson came off the phone she hugged her little girl and said, "I don't know how you knew about Gracie, but you've saved her from something very serious indeed. I'm sorry I didn't take you more seriously when you first spoke to me."

"It's okay, Mummy. Don't thank me; just thank Alice," Kathy beamed.

Mrs Hodson assumed that Alice was one of those imaginary friends that children of Kathy's age sometimes dream up, and she took her daughter upstairs to her bedroom and tucked her in.

Kathy saw the girl in the looking-glass three more times after that eventful winter night. From then on she waited patiently each night to see Alice a fourth time, but the girl from the mirror never visited her again.

THE MEN IN BLACK
Shadowy Visitors Who Stalk UFO Witnesses

In January 1952, Albert K Bender, a dedicated American UFO investigator, founded the International Flying Saucer Bureau in Connecticut. Bender spent an intensive year studying the UFO phenomenon from every conceivable angle, and then, one night, the solution to the enigma hit him. Bender later stated, "I went into the fantastic and came up with the answer."

But no one ever got to know just what this answer was, for according to Bender, he was silenced by three sinister men who appeared in his bedroom one afternoon. The UFO investigator had typed an article about his findings for his own non profit-making journal *Space Review*, when he experienced a sudden dizzy spell. He went upstairs to lie down, and was confronted by the sight of three black silhouettes materialising in his bedroom.

When the shadows became solid, Bender could make out that they were three men dressed in black clothes, their faces partly shaded by the Homburg-style hats that each of them wore. Bender described how he felt the strangers probing his mind, and one of them told him that his speculation about the UFOs was correct. Then Bender noticed that this man in black was holding the typescript of the article he had written for the UFO journal. A strong voice inside Bender's head told him, "You are not to tell anyone the truth; it is your duty as an American citizen. We have a special assignment down here and must not be disturbed by your people.

We are among you and know your every move." Moments later, the odd trio were nowhere to be seen – they had somehow vanished into thin air.

Naturally, Bender was ridiculed when he told his colleagues about the strange visitants but, unknown to most UFO researchers at the time, Bender's encounter with mysterious men in black was by no means a unique occurrence – reports of identically-dressed visitors have been cropping up since the flying saucer era began in 1947. In the early days it was assumed that the strangers were CIA or FBI personnel, because of their clandestine behaviour. In all the early reports, the men in black were said to wear outdated black suits and trilby hats, and were always seen to arrive in a black Cadillac bearing number plates which turned out to be bogus. The visitors' faces, invariably described as 'oriental-looking', were often said to be crudely daubed with makeup. The victims who were harassed by the men in black were always people who had encountered a UFO, and were always alone at the time of the visitation, just like Albert Bender.

In November 1961, office worker Paul Miller and three companions were on a homeward journey to Minot, North Dakota, after a hunting trip, when they noticed a 50-foot-long cylindrical object hovering in a field. The cylinder was glowing with a whitish-green light. Then, two figures descended from the underside of the strange craft. From his stationary car, Paul Miller watched them advance, and panic seized him. He grabbed his rifle, leapt out of the car, and fired at the creatures, wounding one of them. He then jumped back into the car with his friends and, with a screech of tyres, tore away from the area.

When the four men arrived at Minot, they felt strange, and soon learned that they had somehow lost three hours in the course of their journey. Then they started to recall the details of how they had all simultaneously suffered a strange blackout while travelling down a secluded road, but the four men agreed to keep their experience of the UFO encounter a secret.

The next morning, three men arrived, unannounced, at the office where Miller worked. They claimed to be government officials, but made no attempt to show their credentials. They quizzed Miller in private about the UFO encounter which they somehow knew about, but for some reason did not mention the shooting incident. The men – described as dark-skinned and dressed in black – forcibly escorted Miller to his home and demanded to see the clothes he had worn on the previous night. One of the men kept examining the soles of the shoes which Miller had worn on the hunting trip. Miller asked the men how they had found out about the UFO sighting, but he received no reply. After probing the house for an hour, the men suddenly left, leaving Miller feeling utterly confused. Some time later he contacted the Air Force, to see if they could throw any light on the events which had taken place. But they too were in the dark regarding the identity of the visitors.

In August 1965, a Californian highway inspector named Rex Heflin spotted a metallic, disc-shaped object floating across the sky over the Santa Ana freeway. Heflin happened to have a Polaroid camera at hand which he used for his job, and managed to take four photographs of the UFO. The fourth picture revealed a doughnut-shaped ring of smoke, which the UFO had left behind when it manoeuvred off into the heavens.

The sighting attracted widespread media attention, and Heflin received a call from a man who said he was from the North American Air Defence Command (NORAD). An individual in typical 'men in black' attire, turned up at Heflin's home and persuaded him to hand over the Polaroid snaps of the UFO. Fortunately, Heflin had taken the trouble to copy the photographs, because the man in black never returned the original snapshots. NORAD denied any knowledge of the 'representative' who had visited Heflin's home.

Two years later, another suspicious-looking official turned up on Heflin's doorstep one night, and mindful of his last encounter with a dubious visitor, Heflin asked the stranger to show him some form of ID. The stranger presented his credentials: a number of cards and documents which suggested that the caller was a Captain CH Edmonds of the Space Systems Division.

"What's your business?" Heflin asked Edmonds.

"It's about the photographs you took of the UFO. Are you going to try to get the originals of them back?" Edmonds asked.

"No," replied Heflin, and he noticed how his answer seemed to make the visitor smile slightly. Heflin suddenly noticed a black Cadillac parked in the street nearby. A silhouetted figure in the back of the vehicle was pointing a small device at Heflin and the visitor. This device was not unlike a modern camcorder, and Heflin was convinced that he was being filmed with it.

The 'Captain' then started to ask Heflin if he had heard about the so-called Bermuda Triangle. Heflin nodded, but the stranger then digressed into mundane talk, before finally bidding him goodnight.

A subsequent investigation proved that there were actually four Captain CH Edmonds on the Air Force's list of officers, but none of them resembled the man who had visited Heflin, and none of the captains had any connection with the Santa Ana UFO case.

Some time later, Heflin returned home to be told by two of his neighbours that they had seen men in military uniform sneaking around the back of Heflin's house. One of the mystery men seemed annoyed about something and resorted to knocking heavily on the front door of the house – before storming off in a Cadillac. On several occasions, Heflin found that the envelopes containing his mail had been tampered with, and whenever he used his telephone, he heard strange clicks which convinced him that he was being bugged.

Another incident involved Robert Richardson of Toledo, Ohio, who, while driving at night in July 1967, was negotiating a bend in a road when he found himself confronted by a strange circular craft that was blocking the road ahead. He braked as hard as he could, but was unable to stop in time and rammed the unearthly-looking object, which somehow faded away seconds after the impact.

Richardson told the police about the strange collision, but when they accompanied him to the scene of the crash, the officers could only make out the skid-marks of Richardson's car. Not satisfied, Richardson returned alone to the crash-scene the next day, and was surprised to find a small, irregular-shaped lump of metal which looked as if it might have come from the UFO. Richardson informed the Aerial Phenomena Research Organization (APRO) and told them exactly what had happened. A member of APRO recorded the time and date of the alleged incident and filed it away, and Richardson later took the strange lump of metal to them for analysis.

Three days later, at 11pm, two men in their late twenties confronted Richardson at his home and, without identifying themselves, asked a series of questions relating to the UFO encounter. For some unexplained reason, Richardson felt peculiar, and had no desire to ask the visitors for their credentials. The strangers were perfectly pleasant, and when they'd finished with their inquiries, they left the house and climbed into a black 1953 Cadillac. Richardson scribbled down the car's number, but when the registration was checked it was found that no such number had ever been issued in the United States.

A week later, two different men visited Richardson. They had dark complexions, and although one spoke in a perfect English accent, the other had a fainter accent with a slight, but indeterminable, foreign intonation. The men tried to persuade Richardson that he had imagined the UFO, but then later demanded that he hand over the lump of metal. When Richardson told them that APRO had the metal, one of the men in black suddenly adopted a sinister attitude and warned, "If you want your wife to stay as pretty as she is, then you'd better get the metal back."

The scientists at APRO concluded that the metal contained an unusually pure proportion of magnesium and iron, and handed the sample back to Richardson. He waited anxiously for the men in black to return for the metal lump, but they never did.

Another classic men in black incident took place at Maine, USA, in September 1976 at the home of Herbert Hopkins, a 58-year-old doctor and hypnotist who was acting as a consultant on an alleged UFO abduction case. Early in the evening, a man phoned Hopkins and identified himself as the vice-president of the New Jersey UFO Research Organization. The caller asked Hopkins if he could come to his home to discuss the abduction case, as it was of immense interest to him. Dr Hopkins said he was welcome to come over. After putting the receiver down, he walked to the porch of his house – and there was the caller, walking up the porch steps. There was no car to be seen, and even if the man had travelled by car, Hopkins knew that the stranger couldn't possibly have got to the house that fast from any phone (in 1976, personal mobile phones were not in use).

Hopkins later described the caller as looking like an undertaker. The hat, suit, tie and shoes he wore were a funereal black. His shirt was white and his suede gloves were grey. The visitor was admitted to the house, and he and Dr Hopkins had been discussing the abduction case for about 20 minutes, when the visitor suddenly suggested something that made the doctor suspicious. The man in black told Hopkins,

"Erase the tapes you have made of the hypnotic sessions with the UFO witnesses. Have nothing further to do with the case."

The suggestion made the doctor uneasy. The man in black put his gloved hand to his mouth and wiped off what appeared to be a thick layer of lipstick. Upon seeing the red smear on his glove, the stranger quickly removed his gloves and put them in his inside jacket pocket. Hopkins watched in trepidation as the visitor stood up and approached him menacingly.

"You have two coins in your pocket. Give me one of them," he demanded

The doctor reached into his pockets and discovered that the visitor was right – he did indeed have two coins. Hopkins placed one of them on the visitor's outstretched hand. Seconds later, the coin on the man's palm seemed to go out of focus – and then vanished before the doctor's unbelieving eyes.

"Neither you nor anyone else on this planet will ever see that coin again," the man in black said.

A few minutes later, the caller seemed to become unsteady on his feet, and his speech faltered. He enigmatically commented, "My energy is running low . . . must go now . . . goodbye."

The visitor staggered out of the house and descended the porch steps with great difficulty. Out of the corner of his eye Dr Hopkins could see a bluish-white light flashing in the driveway, but he was too afraid to look properly at what it was.

Later that night, when the doctor's family had returned from visiting relatives, one of them noticed strange markings on the driveway. The black streaky markings ran along the centre of the driveway – where no wheels could possibly have been. Stranger still, on the following morning, the markings had vanished, even though there had been no over night rain to wash them away.

Dr Hopkins was naturally reluctant to tell anyone about the bizarre episode, but three days later, on 24 September, the mystery deepened when his daughter-in-law Maureen was also involved in a similar men in black incident.

Maureen received a telephone call from a man who said he was a friend of her husband, and he asked if he and his girlfriend could come to visit. Maureen briefly checked with her husband John who the caller was, and he explained that he had met an odd man a couple of days back at a fast-food restaurant. With some misgivings, Maureen told the caller that he was welcome to come over with his companion.

The couple soon arrived and Maureen observed that they both appeared to be in their mid-thirties, but wore curiously old-fashioned clothes. The woman's breasts were set very low, and she walked in a peculiar way which seemed to be due to a hip problem. Both visitors took slow, short steps, as if they were frightened of falling.

John and Maureen offered them each of them a bottle of cola. The couple accepted the drinks with enthusiastic nods but did not even even bother to taste them.

John and Maureen surveyed the way in which the couple sat awkwardly on the sofa – there was something artificial and robotic about their movements. But they managed to make themselves more than comfortable on the sofa. In fact, they were unable to keep their hands off each other and the man started to rub his partner's breasts with his hands, looking at John as he did so, asking,

"Is this the way it is done?"

John and Maureen were flabbergasted at the man's behaviour.

"Do you and Maureen watch television much?" the man suddenly asked, and stopped fondling his partner.

"Yes, I suppose so. Why?" John answered, now intrigued by the odd pair.

The man continued to quiz them in the most direct manner. Did they read books? What did they read? What did they talk about? As if this were not rude enough, he then put two outrageous questions to Maureen: "Do you have any nude pictures of yourself?" and even more strangely, "How were you made?"

Enough was enough. Maureen stood up and insisted the couple left immediately. The man and woman rose to leave, but the former suddenly seemed unable to walk. His inability to move appeared to frighten the woman, who turned to John and said, "Please move him; I can't move him myself".

But the man suddenly became animated again, and walked directly to the door in a straight line, followed by his female companion. They both left without saying goodbye.

The reports of these strange individuals who pop up at the home and workplace of UFO witnesses are still being reported. The FBI has shown an interest in the men in black phenomenon, and has frequently attempted to track down the impostors – but to date no one has been arrested. The men in black are always one step ahead of the authorities, and they now seem to be changing their mode of transport. The reports of black Cadillacs have now been almost entirely superseded by accounts of black unmarked helicopters buzzing around the neighbourhood of UFO witnesses.

In early 1994, George and Shirley Coyne, directors of the American UFO investigation organization MUFORA, actually presented the FBI with a videotape that clearly shows a black helicopter tailing their car. The couple have allegedly received threats from the men in black, but Shirley Coyne is not worried by them, asserting: "We're not afraid. They haven't done anything to us yet!"

Since the collapse of Communism in the former Soviet Union, the Russians have released many top secret reports of men in black incidents which have occurred in their country. In April 1992, one female witness who observed a UFO at close range near Moscow was later harassed by three mysterious men in black. One of the men actually paralysed the woman simply by touching her. Throughout the intense paralysis, the woman felt as if her mind was being ransacked by the oriental-looking man. For months after the traumatic incident she also exhibited a strange bio-magnetism: pots and pans, anything metal, would stick to her as if she were a magnet, and people who touched her hands often experienced a severe electric shock.

Who are the sinister black-clad stalkers? Suggestions that they are secret servicemen sowing the seeds of disinformation – a typical CIA practice – just don't stand up to scrutiny when we realise that these unearthly thugs have been reported in countries as far afield as Russia and China, where Western intelligence agents cannot operate. This leaves us with only one other possibility: that the men in black are from another planet – perhaps even another dimension. But what is their purpose here on Earth? Only time will tell.

SADHU SUNDAR SINGH
The Holy Man of the Himalayas

In the early 1890s Sundar Singh, a young Indian boy from a wealthy Sikh family, accompanied his deeply religious mother on a visit to a sadhu – a mystic who has opted for a nomadic life in his search for truth. The encounter with the old holy man had a profound effect on young Sundar, and he was soon embarking on his own search for God.

When Sundar's mother and brother died when he was 14, his grief turned to hatred – directed against the Christian missionaries who were visiting India. Sundar detested the Western religion, and he started to demonstrate his hatred by stoning the local Christian preachers. On one occasion, he held a Bible in the air, waved it at the missionaries, then set fire to it.

Three days after this act of denouncement, the embittered teenager prayed all night for a sign from the 'true god'. Suddenly, in the middle of the long prayer session, a vision of Jesus Christ materialised in front of the Indian boy, who almost fainted with fear. The vision said to him,

"How long will you persecute me? I have come to save you. You pray to know the right way. Take it."

The apparition vanished, leaving Sundar elated, but surprised that he had been visited by a Christian god. He looked at the spot where the figure had appeared, shaking his head in disbelief until it dawned on him that his spiritual search was over – he must now preach the Gospel which he had once despised.

In 1905, Sundar was baptised into the Christian Church and took an Anglican ordination course, but he later decided that Anglicanism was too conventional. His new-found faith remained as strong as ever, but he thought the rituals of Anglicanism were not compatible with his Indian traditions and culture, and he was sure he could spread the word of God without the need for a white dog-collar. He regarded himself as a spiritual hybrid – a Christian sadhu, in fact.

Sundar visited Tibet by crossing the Himalayas on foot. He was aware that it was dangerous to preach Christianity in a Buddhist country, and on his third trip across the mountains, he was arrested and condemned to death for trying to convert the Buddhists to his faith. Buddhist law prohibits a true disciple from killing another, so malefactors are usually executed in ways that exonerate adherents of Buddhism from direct responsibility. Sundar was beaten, his clothes ripped from him and finally, he was pushed down a deep dry well. With a sickening squelch he hit the bottom, his landing cushioned by a layer of putrid, decomposing bodies: the carcasses of previous victims. Before he knew it there was a resounding clang, then total darkness. The Buddhists had closed the well's heavy iron lid above him. Now it was only a matter of time – he would surely either starve to death, or be asphyxiated when the air ran out.

Sundar lay there, stunned and bruised from his beating and almost suffocated by the foul stench of rotting flesh. Many would have resigned themselves to certain death in such a gruesome predicament, but Sundar only had to recall the vision of Jesus to allay his fear. Putting his hands together he started to pray fervently, becoming so absorbed that his pain and hunger faded into the background. On the third night the sound of a key rattling in the lock of the iron lid above interrupted his prayers. The metal cover lifted, and a voice boomed down the well: "Seize the rope!"

Sundar peered upwards into the moonlight which now streamed down the well shaft and was soon able to discern a rope with a loop at its end being lowered down towards him. He grabbed it, placed his foot in the loop, and found himself being slowly hauled out of the awful well. Naturally, he could not wait to find out who had saved him, but when he was back above ground, Sundar saw that there was no one at the other end of the rope. He staggered from the area, taking deep, hungry gulps of fresh air, and realised that he had been plucked from the brink of certain death by something unearthly.

The bewildered sadhu rested in some bushes until dawn, then cautiously returned to the local caravansenai (a type of inn where travellers rested), where his inexplicable reappearance caused a sensation. Sundar was promptly arrested and taken to the head Lama, who demanded to know how he had managed to escape from the well. Sundar's account of the paranormal rope trick enraged the Lama, who was convinced that he was lying. He suspected that someone had stolen his key, but on examining the bunch of keys on his girdle, he saw that the key to the well cover was still there; it had never left him, and this so frightened the Lama that he ordered Sundar to leave Tibet immediately.

Sundar continued to have mystical encounters. He claimed to have made contact with a secret Indian Christian sect, whom he urged to declare themselves publicly. He also maintained that he had met a rishi (hermit) who was incredibly old, living in a cave 13,000 feet above sea-level. The old man was an advanced mystic, and was able to impart a series of apocalyptic visions to Sundar, but the sadhu refused to divulge what he had seen.

In the 1920s, Sundar made many trips to Burma, Ceylon, China, Malaysia, America, Japan and Europe. He continued to preach all over the globe, but in 1929, he disappeared without trace in the Himalayas.

RICHARD III
Murderous Uncle or Victim of Tudor Propaganda?

In 1674, workmen demolishing a staircase in the Tower of London's White Tower, discovered a wooden chest buried ten feet deep beneath the staircase. It contained the skeletons of two children, the taller of the two lying on its back and the other lying across it, face down. King Charles II ordered an immediate investigation, and the official examiners concluded that the skeletons were the remains of 12-year-old Edward V and his 10-year-old brother, Richard Duke of York – the two princes who had disappeared in suspicious circumstances at the Tower of London in July 1483.

King Charles had the remains interred in Westminster Abbey in a marble tomb designed by Christopher Wren. In 1933, a pathologist and a dental surgeon were given permission to examine the alleged remains of the princes, and the bones were exhumed.

Pathologist William Wright and dental surgeon George Northcroft were able to determine the ages at death of the skeletons. The investigators could not tell what sex the children were, as they had died before reaching puberty, and the bones were difficult to date, but they seemed to belong to a time period around the 15th century.

The disappearance of the princes in the Tower has been the subject of much debate for hundreds of years. The consensus is that they were murdered by their uncle, Richard III, popularly portrayed (thanks to Shakespeare and Sir Thomas More) as a sadistic, hunch-backed schemer with a twisted mind.

Upon the death of Edward IV in 1483, his brother Richard was appointed Protector of the Realm and guardian of Edward's two sons, the boy, King Edward V and his younger brother Richard, Duke of York. As soon as the preparations for Edward's Coronation were underway in London, Richard rode to Stony Stratford, near Northampton, and escorted Edward to the Tower of London. Edward's younger brother Richard was taken by his mother, Queen Elizabeth Woodville, to Westminster Abbey for sanctuary, but the Queen was later persuaded to let her son join his brother in the Tower.

In June of that year, cleric Ralph Shaw proclaimed that the princes were bastards because Edward IV's marriage to Elizabeth Woodville had been invalid, and so, in the following month, Richard of Gloucester had himself proclaimed as king and was crowned on 6 July. Meanwhile, the princes were still incarcerated in the Tower.

Many were angered by Richard's speedy path to the throne, and most people doubted that the princes were illegitimate. The Duke of Buckingham, who wanted Henry Tudor to be king, led a revolt against Richard, but the rebellion was unsuccessful and the Duke was beheaded for treason. Around the time of the failed insurgency, England was rife with rumours about the princes in the Tower. It was whispered that they had been murdered by the usurper king.

Thirty years after the sinister disappearance of the princes, Sir Thomas More, in his biography of Richard III, claimed that, shortly after his Coronation, the king sent a messenger to the Keeper of the Tower, ordering him to kill the princes, but the keeper, Sir Robert Brackenbury, refused. The king then ordered his protégé, Sir James Tyrell, to do the despicable deed, and after persuading Brackenbury to hand over the keys to the room where the princes were being held, Tyrell put the murderous plan into action.

He instructed his burly housekeeper, John Dighton, and Miles Forest, who had been minding the princes, to kill the boys as they slept. Dighton and Forest crept into the chamber at midnight and swiftly wrapped the princes up in their bedclothes. Dighton pressed their featherbed upon their faces and lay on it until all the violent wriggling and kicking ceased.

According to More, Tyrell then instructed the murderers to bury the suffocated princes at the foot of the stairs in the Tower, under a heap of stones. But how true is More's account? He based his story on an alleged confession to the crime made by Tyrell before his execution in 1502. More was an upholder of the Tudor state, and, as such, was probably using his biography of Richard III to defame him. It was More who claimed that Richard III was 'crooked-backed' and 'ill-featured' – despite the fact that no contemporary portrait of Richard III exists which shows him as ugly or deformed in any way.

Today, historians are still uncertain about the actual fate of the princes. Some believe that they were not murdered at all, but smuggled out of the Tower, probably to spend the rest of their lives in obscurity under assumed names. But if the skeletons were not those of the two princes, whose were they? For years a rumour has persisted that one of the fully-grown princes, Richard of York, is actually depicted as an adult in a Hans Holbein painting of Sir Thomas More and his family. If the princes were not murdered, we are left wondering who the two discovered corpses were.

But if the princes were murdered, is Richard III the only suspect? Someone else who had a strong motive for the double murder was Henry Tudor, who defeated Richard at the Battle of Bosworth Field in 1485 and became Henry VII. Being the great-grandson of Edward III's illegitimate son, Henry was excluded from the succession. His claim to the throne was based only upon the right of conquest, and so, to strengthen his claim, he married Elizabeth of York, sister of the princes in the Tower. He then had his wife declared illegitimate, which meant that her brothers in the Tower were the same, a state of affairs which meant that Henry would have to dispose of the princes if he was to become king. Furthermore, Henry did not claim that Richard III had murdered his nephews until almost a year after Richard's death. When Richard III gained the throne, Henry accused him of tyranny and cruelty – but we'll never know why he didn't accuse Richard of murder at that time.

MICHEL DE NOSTREDAME
The Man Who Saw Tomorrow

Four centuries ago, a French physician sat in his candlelit attic at midnight and stared into a brass bowl of water with a quill in his hand, ready to record the strange moving images which he could just discern on the surface of the bowl's cloudy water. These images were glimpses of future events – great wars, plagues, assassinations, revolutions, and the rise and fall of kings who had not yet been born. The seer was Michel de Nostredame, who is now better known under the Latinised form of his name: Nostradamus.

Because it was the age of the Inquisition, Nostradamus wrote of his weird visions in cryptic verses using quatrains. Hundreds of these quatrains were published in 1555 in a book of prophecy called *Centuries*, which was immediately met with critical acclaim and is still widely read to this day, because of the amazing accuracy of the prophecies. In one quatrain, for example, the prophet gives details of an event some three hundred years before it occurred:

> *Pasteur will be celebrated as* ꜰ
> *a god-like figure.*
> *This is when the Moon completes*
> *her great cycle.*

Louis Pasteur, the great French chemist, founded the Pasteur Institute in 1889 – the year in which a lunar cycle was actually completed.

In another quatrain, the 16th century oracle apparently foresees the abdication of Edward VIII:

For not wanting to consent to the divorce,
Which afterwards will be recognised as unworthy,
The king of the islands will be forced to flee,
And one put in his place who has no sign of kingship.

In 1936, Edward VIII was forced to abdicate because he wanted to marry American divorcee, Mrs Wallis Simpson. The one 'put in his place' was, of course, Edward's younger brother George VI, who did indeed lack experience of 'kingship'.

The following quatrain gives an uncanny account of Adolf Hitler:

In the mountains of Austria near the Rhine
There will be born of simple parents
A man who will claim to defend Poland and Hungary
And whose fate shall never be certain.

The last line of the quatrain unequivocally refers to the unidentifiable charred body found in the Berlin bunker which was assumed to be Hitler's. After World War Two, there were many who believed that Hitler had really escaped from Berlin and fled to South America with Martin Bormann and Josef Mengele.

In another extraordinary verse, Nostradamus almost names the dictator:

Beasts wild with hunger will cross rivers,
The greatest part of the battlefield
Will be against Hister.

Perhaps the most fascinating quatrains are the ones which seem to echo recent events. The following example predicts the fall of a 'wall in the East' – perhaps the Berlin Wall, which has indeed now fallen:

The royal bird over the city of the Sun
Will give a nightly warning for seven months
The Wall in the East will fall
Thunder and lightning, in seven days.

The last line may refer to the amazing pace of events during that historic week in November 1989, when the notorious barrier was demolished and Berlin ceased to be a divided city overnight.

Nostradamus may have also foreseen the Russo-American alliance initiated by Presidents Gorbachev and Bush against the Iraqi leader Saddam Hussein:

One day, the two great leaders will be friends
Their great power will be seen to grow.
The New Land will be at the height of its power
To the Man of Blood, the number is reported.

The 'New Land' was the name of America in Nostradamus's day. The 'Man of Blood' is identified by Nostradamus in other quatrains as the third and final anti-Christ (Napoleon and Hitler being the first and second). Nostradamus prophesied that this anti-Christ would rise in the Middle East, near the rivers of the Tigris and Euphrates – the same two rivers that course through Iraq into the Persian Gulf.

According to Nostradamus, the Man of Blood will be an Arab and 'a strong master of Mohammedan Law', and the war against him will begin with a short battle – perhaps the Gulf War of the early 1990s? But Nostradamus continues, stating that the Arab will hold out for 27 years and resort to using a 'horror cloud' – which sounds suspiciously like a chemical weapon. Let us hope Nostradamus was wrong on this occasion.

MOTHER SHIPTON
The White Witch of Yorkshire

In July 1488, the midwife tending Agatha Southiel as she gave birth, was in for a nasty shock. As the nurse cut the umbilical chord and tied up the loose ends, the newborn babe started to chuckle. Simultaneously, the raging thunderstorm outside came to an abrupt end, and the murky skies over the North Yorkshire town of Knaresborough turned to a delightful azure as the sun reappeared. A group of Agatha's neighbours who had also watched the strange birth, exchanged frightened glances. As if at an invisible signal, everyone present, including the midwife, suddenly made a mad dash out of the cottage, leaving poor Agatha and her freakish baby daughter to look after themselves.

Rampant rumours began to circulate in the tight-knit market town about the birth of 'the Devil's child' and 'Lucifer's daughter' and Agatha Southiel was soon shunned by everyone who knew of the strange 'laughing baby'. Backs were resolutely turned on the woman who was thought to have copulated with Satan, and in the end, the malicious gossipers drove Agatha into the sanctuary of a convent. The care of the unfortunate infant who had been the talk of the town –

Janet Ursula Southiel – was handed over to a nurse and she decided to delete the child's first name.

When little Ursula Southiel began school, she was taunted by her classmates for having no parents, but she did not allow their cruel jibes to upset her; she simply set her invisible 'demon friend' on her classmates, and he, or rather 'it', would bite, punch and pinch them. The unseen companion – naturally presumed to be Old Nick himself – didn't exactly make the schoolmaster feel comfortable, and he quickly made it clear that Ursula was no longer welcome at the school.

Snubbed by every school she was sent to, the witch-girl spent most of her days in solitude with only the company of her supernatural playmate. But her lonely days ended in her early teens when she met a young carpenter named Tobias Shipton. It was love at first sight, and the two sweethearts were soon married. After which, the newly-weds moved to Skipton, about 35 miles west of York.

It was here that Ursula discovered that she had the ability to look into the future. She accurately foresaw Henry VIII's invasion of France in 1513, and correctly predicted that the 'English Lion' (Henry again) would defeat the 'Lillies' (the French), and that the 'Princely Eagle' (Maximillian of Hapsburg) would join the Lion in the battle. She also predicted that the English Cavalry would 'cause great shame unto' the French, and was correct in this prediction, for the French retreated so fast from the English cavalry that the short-lived military encounter was later known as the Battle of the Spurs.

In the year 1530, Ursula predicted that 'The Mitred Peacock' (Cardinal Wolsey) would hide out from trouble with Henry VIII by trying to escape to York, but would never live to enter the city. News of this prophecy spread through most of the villages of England until it reached the ears of Wolsey himself. The Cardinal was intrigued; his relationship with the king was shaky to say the least, and so, keen to see if the 'Yorkshire Witch' could gain knowledge about the king's court, he sent three spies to Ursula Shipton's home. They were the Duke of Suffolk, Lord Darcy and Lord Percy, and they wore disguises for the assignment. A Yorkshire man named Beasley accompanied the noblemen as a guide.

When the four men arrived at Ursula's cottage, Beasley knocked on the door and the prophetess answered.

"Come in Mr Beasley, and the three noble Lords with you," said Ursula.

Beasley and the three noblemen were stunned at Ursula's knowledge of their identities. The four men entered the house and Ursula treated them to delicious oatcakes and ale. The Duke of Suffolk asked Ursula if she had really said that Cardinal Wolsey would never see York.

"No, I said he might see the city but never enter it," Ursula replied, as she sat studying the flames of the blazing fire.

"When he comes to York he will surely burn thee," the Duke of Suffolk warned.

At this, Ursula suddenly threw a linen handkerchief onto the fire and said, "If this burns, so shall I."

The four visitors watched the piece of linen intensely. It rested on an incandescent log, and the flames licked at it, but 15 minutes later, Ursula cackled to herself and lifted the piece of linen out of the fire with a poker. The cloth hadn't been touched by the flames. This so impressed the noblemen, that one of them asked Ursula to tell them their fortunes. She pointed to the Duke of Suffolk.

"My love, the time will come when you will be as low as I am, and I am a low one indeed," she said.

The Duke was naturally puzzled and not a little alarmed by the witch's words, but years later, in 1554, the Duke of Suffolk was beheaded for treason, and was thus made a 'low one' when his severed head lay on the ground.

To Lord Percy, Ursula said, "Show your horse in the quick, and you do well, but your body will be buried in York pavement and your head shall be stolen from the bar and carried into France."

Lord Percy was beheaded in 1572 and, as Ursula predicted, his head was impaled on a pole over the Michelgate Bar Gate at York, and later stolen by a Catholic fanatic and taken to France.

Finally, to Lord Darcy, the seeress pronounced, "You have made a great gun! Go and shoot it off, for it will do you no good. You are going to war, and you will pain many a man, but you will kill none."

Being a soldier as well as a statesman, Darcy was concerned with artillery, but all the guns he commanded could not save him when he participated in the Pilgrimage of Grace – a revolt in northern England against the severe economic and religious hardline reforms of Henry VIII's government. Darcy was one of the 230 men who were beheaded because of their part in the 1536 uprising.

As for Cardinal Wolsey, Ursula was correct yet again. He did travel towards York, but only got as far as Cawood, eight miles from his intended destination. There, Lord Northampton apprehended him and presented him with an arrest warrant. Wolsey was charged with high treason and taken to London to be incarcerated in the Tower until execution, but died on the road to the capital.

Ursula – known in her later years as Mother Shipton – died peacefully in her bed at the age of 73 in 1561. It is alleged that she often quoted the following rhyme, which is said to prophesy the arrival of the automobile, radio, submarine, train, aeroplane, steamship … and also, the end of the World:

Carriages without horses shall go,
And accidents fill the world with woe.
Around the Earth thoughts shall fly,
In the twinkling of an eye.
The world upside down shall be
And gold found at the root of a tree.
Through the hills man shall ride,
And no horse shall be at his side.
Under water men shall walk,
Shall ride, shall sleep, shall even talk.
In the air men shall be seen,
In white, in black, in green;
Iron in the water shall float,
As easily as a wooden boat.
To an end the world shall come,
In the year two thousand and sixty-one.

PYOTR ILYICH TCHAIKOVSKY
Was the Great Russian Composer Murdered?

Pyotr Ilyich Tchaikovsky was born on 7 May 1840 at Kamsko-Votinsk (about 100 miles north-east of Izhevsk), where his father was an inspector of the government mines. From an early age it was evident that Tchaikovsky was musically talented, and he was encouraged to develop his gift, but after the family moved to St Petersburg, young Tchaikovsky entered the School of Jurisprudence and became a civil servant. He finally enrolled at the recently-opened Conservatoire of Music in St Petersburg in 1862, and after three years he was employed by Nicholas Rubinstein, his previous orchestration tutor, to teach music at a conservatoire in Moscow. He became a professor there in 1866.

Tchaikovsky was constantly prone to long bouts of debilitating depression, and was forever 'recognising' his weak points. He once said, "I cannot complain of lack of inventive power, but I have always suffered from want of skill in the management of form."

At the age of 37, he was confronted with the persistent sexual advances of one of his pupils, Antonina Ivanovna Miliukova, a 28-year-old nymphomaniac and borderline psychopath. The composer, a repressed homosexual, despised his own sexuality at the time, and dreaded being found out, but he was forced to admit to Antonina that he was unsuitable for her because he was only interested in his own sex. But after Antonina had pleaded long and hard for his love, and threatened to commit suicide if he turned his back on her, he finally consented to marry her.

The unconsummated marriage lasted for just one miserable month, after which Tchaikovsky left his bride and suffered a nervous breakdown. In an attempt to end his life he walked into an icy river one night and stood waist deep in the waters, praying for pneumonia to overtake him. His failed attempt at suicide left him feeling even more wretched and, in total despair, he sought refuge from Antonina in the home of his brother, Anatol. Here, his health deteriorated even more rapidly, and he subsequently slipped into a coma which lasted two days. In the end, Antonina accepted the abandonment and tried to find solace with a string of lovers. She bore at least five children by various men and ended up in a lunatic asylum, where she died, in 1917.

Tchaikovsky had confided to close friends that the only woman he had ever loved was his mother, who had died when the composer was 14. Her death had had such a profound effect on him that many surmised, rather unreasonably, that the shock of her demise had been a contributing factor to his homosexuality.

After a recuperative period abroad, Tchaikovsky resigned from the conservatoire and retired into the country to devote himself entirely to composition. He made occasional trips abroad, and was made an Honorary Doctor of Music of Cambridge University in 1893. Shortly after returning from England in the October of that year, Tchaikovsky conducted his first performance of his *Symphony No. 6 in B Minor* at St Petersburg. The *Pathétique Symphony*, so called because of its melancholic mien, was not received well by the critics.

Tchaikovsky's depression deepened, but two days after the *Pathétique* première, his grand opera, *Eugene Onegin* was greeted with a standing ovation. The composer suddenly seemed on top of the world again. He enjoyed meals out with friends and even visited the theatre. But a week later, a Reuters telegram from St Petersburg stunned the musical world. It read:

M. Tschaikowsky [sic], the famous composer, died here at 3 o'clock this morning from the effects of cholera. On Saturday evening he dined at a restaurant in the city, and drank some water which had not previously been boiled. Symptoms of cholera showed themselves on Sunday, and although every effort was made by the doctors in attendance to stay the progress of the disease, M. Tschaikowsky's condition became rapidly worse. He lost consciousness yesterday afternoon.

The musical genius who had composed the *1812 Overture* and the music for *Swan Lake, The Sleeping Beauty* and *The Nutcracker Suite,* had allegedly died of Asiatic cholera at the age of 53. He passed away after four days of acute vomiting, diarrhoea and convulsions, at his brother's apartment at Number 13 Dzerzhinsky Street, St Petersburg.

The great writer Leo Tolstoy and Tchaikovsky's composer-friend Rimsky-Korsakov were very sceptical of the cholera story. In his memoirs, Korsakov states that Tchaikovsky's death 'occasioned all kinds of gossip' and an article in a newspaper of the day reported: 'Contradictory rumours are afloat with regard to the causes of Tchaikovsky's illness.' The article goes on in a tantalising manner, skirting around the murmurs of murder and tales of a cover-up surrounding the the composer's untimely death.

The body of Tchaikovsky lay in state in an open coffin for two days. Those who came to pay their last respects noted the serene face of the composer, and some thought that his features were too tranquil-looking for a man who had died of cholera; it was more usual for the face of a cholera victim to be contorted and twisted from an agonising death. Official regulations adamantly stated that all cholera victims were to be kept in a closed coffin and buried immediately, so Korsakov also thought it strange that the corpse of a man who had died of such an infectious disease should be laid out in an open coffin, in clear breach of Russian health regulations.

Tolstoy wrote of the composer's mysterious death: 'I am very sorry for Tchaikovsky – as a man about whom something is not quite clear – even more than as a musician. It's too neat and tidy; it's natural, yet not natural.'

Was Tolstoy intimating that Tchaikovsky was murdered? Although the composer was sneeringly regarded by his countrymen as something of a renegade cosmopolitan, lacking in nationalistic pride, Tchaikovsky had no real enemies to contend with in the musical sphere. So how do we explain the following?

Thirty years after Tchaikovsky's death, Dr Lev Bertenson – the man who had been the personal physician to Tsar Alexander III – was on his deathbed when he summoned his son, Nikolay, and told him a dark secret. Dr Bertenson told Nikolay that he had been the senior doctor attending Tchaikovsky as he lay dying. Dr Bertenson told his son that the great composer had not died from cholera at all – but had actually poisoned himself with an arsenical preparation. According to the dying doctor, Tchaikovsky had been pressurised into 'doing the decent thing' to avoid disgrace. Bertenson's deathbed revelation was backed up by Nikolay Jacobi – the lawyer to the Tsar. According to Jacobi, Tchaikovsky was infatuated with the handsome nephew of Count Stenbok Fermor. The Count was outraged by the homosexual composer's interest in his nephew and wrote to the Tsar, who feared the matter would prove to be an embarrassment to his court. So Tsar Alexander III put the composer before a kangaroo court. Tchaikovsky was found guilty of having a homosexual lust for Count Stenbok – Fermor's nephew, and was ordered to take arsenic.

What are we to make of the suspicions of Tolstoy and Korsakov, and the apocryphal tales posthumously credited to Dr Bertenson and Nikolay Jacobi? Did Tchaikovsky commit suicide, or was he murdered? Perhaps the composer anticipated the ceaseless delving into his suspicious death when he wrote: 'The notion that some day people will try to probe into the private world of my thoughts and feelings, into everything that I have so carefully hidden throughout my life, is very sad and unpleasant.'

ROBIN HOOD
Who Was the Legendary Outlaw?

Way back in the 13th century, when England was a land of sprawling wild forests where deer, wolves, bears and wild boars roamed, there lived a curious individual named Robin Hood, who was said to be an outlaw. In those times the word 'outlaw' didn't just mean a criminal living outside of the law, but someone who had become an outcast of society, because of a wrong committed against the king.

The earliest record of the Robin Hood legend is a tome printed in 1420 by Wynkyn de Worde entitled, *A Lytell Geste of Robyn Hode*. According to this early book, Little John was not the giant outlaw with whom we are familiar, but merely a medium-sized Lytell John, meaning his family name was Lytell. The merry men mentioned in de Worde's text aren't merry, either. In those days 'merry' simply meant that the story had a happy ending, but down the centuries the word has become confused with the carefree, living-off-the-land philosophy of Robin's men.

In the 15th century story, Robin's enemy, the Sheriff of Nottingham, is said to be the king's representative, responsible for keeping law and order over an area stretching from Nottinghamshire and southern Yorkshire to the coast, and true to the modern legend, the Sheriff gets steamed up at the mere mention of Robin Hood's name.

By the 19th century, most antiquarians regarded Robin Hood as a mere invention of the mediaeval story-tellers, but the English historian and Shakespearean scholar Joseph Hunter thought otherwise, and decided to appoint himself to the task of unearthing historical evidence to prove that the famous outlaw had existed. Hunter combed the catalogues of the Historic Documents Commission, which covered 800 years of British history, and at the end of his mammoth quest, in 1852, he caused a furore among his fellow historians when he announced that he had found concrete evidence to show, beyond doubt, that Robin Hood had been a real flesh and blood individual.

Hunter had found the record of a boy named Robert Hood who was born in the town of Wakefield in Yorkshire between 1285 and 1295. Robert's father was Adam Hood, a forester in the service of the Earl de Warenne, Lord of the Manor of Wakefield. Robert Hood married a maiden named Matilda, who is recorded as having been brought before a court for taking dry wood from an old oak tree. She was fined twopence.

In the year 1316, Robert and Matilda bought a piece of Earl de Warenne's land for the sum of two shillings to build a house on. According to another record, Robert's landlord in the year 1322 was Thomas, Earl of Lancaster. This Earl called upon all his tenants to rebel against King Edward II, and as Robert was one of the nobleman's tenants, he went into battle for him, and the record says Robert Hood was very useful in the rebellion because of his amazing skill at archery. Nevertheless, the rebellion failed and the Earl of Lancaster was beheaded for treason. The Earl's estates were then forfeited to the king and Robert Hood and the other survivors of the failed insurrection became outlaws and fled for the cover of Barnsdale Forest in southern Yorkshire. The southern end of this forest adjoined Sherwood Forest.

So was Joseph Hunter right? Had he found positive proof of Robin's existence? No one can be sure, for there are records of other candidates who could be the real Robin Hood. One is Robert Hood of Cirencester, an outlaw who was wanted for murder around the year 1213, and there is another Robin Hood who went to prison in 1354 for offences he committed in Rockingham Forest. Then again there is the record of a Robert Hode, an outlaw of York in 1225. Unlike Robert Hood of Wakefield, none of these candidates lived in close proximity to Sherwood Forest, and none of them was skilled in archery, so there is a strong case for Joseph Hunter's claim.

CHARLES WALTON
The Strange Case of the Witch Murder in Shakespeare Country

In his book, *The Anatomy of Crime*, the celebrated Superintendent Robert Fabian of Scotland Yard, one of the most hard-boiled, logical and scientific detectives in the history of criminology, wrote a curious paragraph about one particular murder case that he never solved:

> *I advise anybody who is tempted at any time to venture into Black Magic, witchcraft, Shamanism – call it what you will – to remember Charles Walton and to think of his death, which was clearly the ghastly climax of a pagan rite. There is no stronger argument for keeping as far away as possible from the villains with their swords, incense and mumbo-jumbo. It is prudence on which your future peace of mind and even your life could depend.*

In this warning to the idly curious, Fabian was referring to the baffling case of the 'Pitchfork Murder', which occurred in 1945 in the village of Lower Quinton, just a few miles south of Stratford-upon-Avon. But before we look into the murder mystery, we must go back in time to 1662, to understand why the area around the scene of the crime is so steeped in witchcraft.

In the spring of 1662, a Scottish witch named Isobel Gowdie was burned at the stake for using a team of harnessed toads to pull a miniature plough across a field. In Celtic mythology, the toad had always been associated with witchcraft, sorcery, curses and blights, and these myths were carried over into Christianity. In Greek lore, Amerindian legend, and even Chinese mythology, the toad was also regarded as a magical creature identified with the powers of darkness, so nobody in 17th century Scotland thought it was strange to put an old woman to death for employing toads to pull a toy plough.

Throughout the rest of Britain, the toad was a much maligned yet respected creature. In the English Fens, for example, a peculiar Roman tradition of using a toad as a compass is still extant. This custom dates back to the days when the occupying Romans would place a dagger on a toad's back, then watch the creature move around slowly until it stopped, when the dagger pointed due north.

Over two centuries after the execution of Isobel Gowdie, another old woman who was suspected of being a witch was also killed. She was 75-year-old Ann

Tenant of Long Compton in Warwickshire, and the man who slayed her was a mentally retarded youth named John Heywood, referred to locally as the village idiot. Heywood was convinced that Miss Tenant was a member of a coven of witches who held their sabbath rituals in the countryside around the village of Long Compton. Some said the old woman also used toads to blight crops by black magic rituals. At the murder trial Heywood confessed, "Her was a proper witch. I pinned her to the ground [with a pitchfork] before slashing her throat with a bill-hook to carve a cross."

Local gossip at the time of the trial had it that Long Compton was becoming the epicentre of witchcraft in the region, and an old saying of the day was: 'There are enough witches in Long Compton to draw a wagonload of hay up Long Compton Hill'. Strangely enough, just south of the village stands a circle of Neolithic or Bronze Age stones known as the Rollright Stones which have been associated with pagan rituals for centuries. Even today, modern witches and occultists still gather within the circle of stones to conduct esoteric rites.

About 15 miles north of the Rollright Stones, the picturesque village of Lower Quinton sits in the shadow of Meon Hill. Even today, Lower Quinton has a spooky aura about it after dark, and is surrounded by eerily-named places such as Devil's Elbow and Upper Slaughter. In a thatched cottage at Lower Quinton in the 1940s, there lived 74-year-old Charles Walton and his unmarried niece, Edith. In his younger days, Walton had worked as a ploughman, but now in old age he was plagued with stabbing rheumatism, and eked out a living putting in a seven-hour day for one shilling and sixpence an hour hedge-cutting for local farmers. He was a familiar figure in the village, with his double-pronged hay-fork over his shoulder and his slash-hook in his hand, hobbling to work up Meon Hill. Outwardly there was nothing to suggest that the old hedger and ditcher was anybody out of the ordinary, but Walton had quite a sinister reputation in the village, where it was common knowledge that he bred huge toads and had once been a legendary horse whisperer.

Horse whispering is the ancient and now largely forgotten art of controlling a horse from a distance without any word or command, using a slight gesture of the hand to make the horse stay, run, canter or gallop. Walton's horse whispering ability seemed nothing short of witchcraft, and his power over animals allegedly extended to cattle, toads and birds. What's more, it was said that Walton had been seen on many occasions imitating the songs of the nightingale and chirping to other species of bird. He openly professed to be conversant in the language of his feathered friends, and they seemed to obey his requests to refrain from eating the seeds sown in the fields of his little plot.

On the morning of 14 February 1945, Charles Walton left home and hobbled up Meon Hill to attend to the hedges which formed the border of Alfred Potter's farm, about a mile from Walton's cottage. At six o'clock that evening, Edith began to worry about her uncle. He still hadn't returned, and he was usually back before four o'clock. She felt sure that something had happened to him, and suspected that the old man might have collapsed as he had recently been complaining about the unbearable rheumatic pain that was crippling his legs.

Edith sought out her neighbour Harry Beasley, and they both hiked up Meon's Hill to Potter's farm – known as 'The Firs' – with a growing sense of foreboding. Farmer Potter told Edith and Harry that he had seen someone in the distance earlier in the day who appeared to be cutting hedges, and had assumed it was Walton. However, Potter thought that Walton had long gone home. He fetched a flashlight and accompanied Walton's niece and her neighbour over the fields to the spot where the old man had last been seen.

The beam of the flashlight revealed the whole horrific scene. Under a willow tree on Meon Hill lay the spread-eagled body of Charles Walton. Potter glanced at the corpse then shielded Edith from the gruesome sight with his arm and took her home. He then summoned the police.

Meanwhile, back at the scene of the crime, Harry Beasley stood guard over his murdered neighbour. He saw that Walton had been impaled with his own pitchfork and that the twin prongs of the tool had been driven through his neck with such force, that they had penetrated the ground to a depth of six inches. Crosses had been carved on Walton's cheeks, neck and abdomen, and the bill-hook that had been used to cut out the symbols, was still wedged between his ribs. Near to the body lay the old man's walking-stick, covered in blood because it had been used to bludgeon his head. His face was frozen in an expression of sheer terror.

The Warwickshire police force reacted strangely to the crime. They seemed to be reluctant to undertake the investigation, and called instead for a murder squad from Scotland Yard to look into the strange killing. On the following day, Detective Superintendent Robert Fabian and his assistant, Detective Sergeant Albert Webb, turned up at the village and were greeted with what appeared to be a conspiracy of silence.

The few locals who would speak, merely told Fabian that Walton had been a strange, secretive old man who bred large natterjack toads in the damp undergrowth of his garden. Fabian also learned that Walton had never been over-fond of company, buying cider by the gallon from pubs and drinking it alone by his kitchen fireside. Fabian could not allow his reasoning to be clouded by super-situation, yet he felt that Walton had probably been ritually murdered and took the unprecedented step of consulting Dr Margaret Murray, a witchcraft expert. Fabian also delved into the local history of the area and was intrigued to uncover a record of the 1875 murder of Ann Tenant, who had been killed in a very similar manner to Charles Walton. Fabian began to suspect that the person or persons who had killed Walton had carried out the murder in order to purge the village of a man regarded as a practising witch.

The line of inquiry then switched to the prisoner-of-war camp over at Long Marston, where Italian, German and Slavonic soldiers were quizzed, but Fabian was confident that the POWs were innocent of Walton's murder.

Then something weird happened. A black dog was found hanged on Meon Hill. There were hushed claims in the village that the hound had been Walton's 'familiar' – a demon in disguise. Even the secular-minded Fabian was unnerved by the hanged dog, for on the first day of the murder investigation, he had climbed Meon Hill to examine the crime scene, and been intrigued to notice a large black retriever seated on a nearby wall, watching him intently. Seconds afterwards, a boy walked past, and Fabian asked him, "Are you looking for your dog?"

The boy returned a blank stare and said, "What dog?"

Fabian then noticed that the dog had vanished, and the boy fled down the hill in absolute terror. He later told the villagers that Fabian had seen a ghostly black dog, which was regarded as a potent of death or bad luck.

Shortly after the hanged dog was cut down from the tree, another dog was run over by a police car, and a spate of other inexplicable canine deaths followed during the murder investigation. As if to underline the relevance of the canine coincidences, Fabian's attention was drawn to a curious passage from an old yellowed book entitled *Folklore, Old Customs and Superstitions in Shakespeare Land*, written in 1930. The text of the passage actually referred to Charles Walton:

At Alveston a ploughman named Charles Walton met a dog on his way home nine times in successive evenings. He told both the shepherd and the carter with whom he worked, and was laughed at for his pains. On the ninth encounter a headless lady rushed past him in a silk dress, and on the next day he heard of his sister's death.

Fabian and Webb learned from several of the more talkative villagers that in early spring 1944, crops had been slow in growing, and there had been several fatal accidents with livestock. The harvest was a disaster and even the beer had turned unaccountably sour in every local pub. Many thought that Walton was the source of the widespread bad luck, so Fabian easily deduced that the old man had been killed to put an end to his evil magical influences. That killer, or killers, had probably had an intimate knowledge of the occult and planned the murder months in advance. Fabian knew that the date of Walton's death – 14 February – was Valentine's Day, and occasionally Ash Wednesday also fell on that date, but 14 February also had a special relevance to the ancient Druids – they carried out human sacrifices on that day to procure a good harvest.

Fabian of the Yard finally had to concede defeat. Four thousand statements had been taken and painstakingly cross-referenced, 29 samples of blood, skin, and hair had been analysed, all to no avail, and the silence in the village remained impenetrable to the London policemen. Fabian and Webb reluctantly retreated to the capital, where more mundane crimes demanded their attention. But for many years afterwards, Robert Fabian returned to Lower Quinton on the anniversary of the killing and hid himself on Meon Hill to keep a watch on the area, perhaps hoping that the murderer would return to the scene of the crime, but he never did.

Speaking of the Walton murder to a newspaper in 1976, the then retired Fabian told a reporter: "Detectives deal in facts, but I must admit there was something uncanny about that investigation."

ADOLF HITLER
Was the Führer a Black Magician?

According to the unfinished manuscript *I Married Hitler's Brother*, which was discovered in the main branch of New York Public Library in the late 1970s, Adolf Hitler had once lodged at a house in the Toxteth district of Liverpool, from November 1912 to April 1913. Historians quickly presumed the manuscript was a hoax, but as they read through the work, many of them concluded that the claims it contained were not as bizarre as they had initially thought.

The author of the controversial manuscript was one Bridget Hitler, the wife of Adolf's half-brother Alois. Irish-born, Bridget's maiden name had been Dowling, and she had met Alois Hitler at the annual Dublin Horse Show of 1909. Dressed in a brown suit and a Homburg hat, the debonair Austrian introduced himself to 17-year-old Bridget in broken English, and it was one of those supposedly rare cases of love at first sight. Bridget began to date the foreigner, who claimed to be in the hotel business, but her parents didn't approve of Alois, and they were shocked to discover that Alois's claim to be in the hotel business meant in fact that he was merely a waiter at the nearby Shelbourne Hotel. This was the final straw, and Bridget's parents demanded an end to the relationship. But Bridget was in love and she eloped with her sweetheart and married him in London.

A year after the marriage, Bridget bore Alois a son, and he was named William Patrick. Bridget later addressed her son as Pat, while Alois called him Willie. In their second year of married life, the couple decided to move to Liverpool, where they opened a small restaurant in the bustling thoroughfare of Dale Street, but it was only a modest success. Alois was a restless person, and he decided to sell the restaurant in order to buy a boarding-house in another part of the city. But the boarding-house venture was an utter disaster, and Alois became bankrupt.

However, his economic outlook improved shortly afterwards, when he won a fortune from backing the winner of the Grand National Steeplechase. Alois used the money to set himself up in the safety-razor business. He decided he needed a partner, so he wrote to his brother-in-law, Anton Raubal, in Vienna, asking him and his wife to come to Liverpool straightaway, and enclosed the travelling expenses.

On a cold November morning in 1912, Alois and Bridget went to Liverpool's Lime Street Station and waited for the 11.30 train to steam in. When the train arrived, the couple waited with bated breath for Anton and his wife to disembark, but they were disappointed. The outline of a solitary figure descending from the carriage was barely visible through the cloud of steam drifting across the platform. A pale-faced young man in a worn-out suit approached and offered his hand to Alois. It was Adolf, his younger half-brother. He explained that he had come in the place of Anton Raubal, who had not been able to make the journey for various reasons. A heated discussion in German broke out between the brothers, and Bridget was so embarrassed by the confrontation, that she left them squabbling on the platform and went home.

In the evening, Alois brought Adolf to his three-bedroomed flat at 102 Upper Stanhope Street, and seeing that the brothers were now on friendlier terms, Bridget cooked dinner for them. After the meal, Adolf retired to the drawing room, while Bridget scolded her husband for giving his brother such a rough reception. Alois said that Adolf – whom he referred to as 'my artist brother' – had deserted from the Austrian army and had been on the run for 18 months. It was when he had confessed this at the station, that Alois had lost his temper.

At that time in Vienna, there was a rigid system of registration of domicile, and this system made it easy to locate anyone failing to report for military service. Alois told Bridget that Adolf had got round this by using the identity papers of his dead brother Edmund. But when the Viennese police finally tracked him down, Adolf fled to Liverpool after begging Anton Raubal's wife for the travelling expenses that Alois had sent to her husband.

Now that Alois had explained the facts, Bridget understood why her husband had made such a scene at the station. According to Bridget, her 23-year-old brother-in-law spent most of his time lounging around the house and playing with two-year-old William Patrick. At first, he hardly spoke to her, but gradually, as the weeks went by, Adolf became friendlier and began talking about his interest in painting and his future plans. He told Bridget how disappointed he was when his application to become an artist at the Academy of Art in Vienna was turned down by a Jewish professor who said that he couldn't paint, but had a minor talent for architecture.

Another subject young Adolf discussed – or rather, argued about – with his sister-in-law, was Germany's future. It was Adolf's unshakeable belief that Germany would one day take its rightful position in the world, and whenever he talked about the 'Fatherland', he would unfold a map of the world that belonged to Alois, spread it across the floor, and explain how Germany would first conquer France, and then England. Sometimes Adolf would disrupt Bridget's housework to discuss his political predictions, and on one occasion when Bridget became so irritated by his ranting that she carried on cleaning, Adolf began to scream and shout at her for ignoring him. Bridget retaliated by telling Adolf that he would never live to see England destroyed by Germany, and added that he wasn't even German – just a low-living Austrian deserter. Hitler was so taken aback by Bridget's riposte that, for once, he became speechless, and began to shake violently as he swelled with anger.

One day, Alois took Adolf on a day trip to London, where Adolf became captivated by the various architectural styles of the city's buildings and landmarks. He was enchanted by the dome of St Paul's Cathedral, and the workings of Tower Bridge. On the train back to Liverpool, the future dictator made several sketches of an enormous version of St Paul's, and rambled on about his magnificent dream of building a domed temple to outlive the Pyramid of Cheops, but Alois fell asleep.

In her controversial manuscript, Bridget mentions a Mrs Prentice – a neighbour who was interested in astrology and the occult. Adolf allegedly spent hours in her home having his cards and horoscopes read. He was enthralled by her prediction that a tremendous future lay ahead of him. Mrs Prentice looked at the Austrian's palm and told him he had a prominent line of destiny, which indicated that he would have a phenomenal career. However, Mrs Prentice also noted that Adolf's heart line crossed his destiny line, which meant that his life's goal could be thwarted by his own emotions, if they got the better of him.

Adolf eventually outstayed his welcome, and Alois insisted that he returned home. So, in May 1913, Adolf left England and returned to Germany. Bridget says in her manuscript that she blamed herself for turning loose a man who plunged the world into its deadliest war.

Many historians who have analysed the manuscript believe that Adolf's trip to Liverpool is entirely credible, and furthermore, November 1912 to May 1913 is something of a lost period in the Führer's life. Hitler never mentioned his stay in Liverpool in *Mein Kampf*, but that could be because he didn't want to publicise his shameful days as a draft-dodging drop-out. Ironically, the last bombs to fall on Liverpool demolished the house in Upper Stanhope Street where Hitler once lived.

Hitler returned to Vienna, where he lived on his wits and made a precarious living selling below-average postcard sketches, beating carpets and doing any odd jobs that came his way. He lived in a doss-house, infested with lice, and wore a long, shabby, black overcoat given to him by a sympathetic Jewish tailor. To escape the cold, Adolf would often wander through the corridors of the Hofburg Museum, where one particular exhibit never failed to mesmerise him: the Holy Lance. This was said to be the very spear which pierced Christ's side when he had yielded up his ghost on the cross. According to legend, the 'Spear of Destiny' as it was called, belonged to the Roman soldier Longinius, who smote Jesus. And in the romance of King Arthur, the merchant Joseph of Aramathea is said to have brought the spear to Britain, where Sir Balim the Savage used it to wound King Pelham. It then went to Austria, and somehow wound up in the Hofburg Museum as part of the Hapsburg regalia. Hitler was well-read, and he knew the biblical reference about the spear from John 19: 33-37 by heart:

But when they came to Jesus, and saw that he was dead already, they broke not his legs: But one of the soldiers with a spear pierced his side, and forthwith came there out blood and water. And he saw it bare record, and his record is true: and he knoweth that he saith true, that ye might believe. For these things were done that the scripture should be fulfilled, a bone of him shall not be broken. And again another scripture saith: They shall look on him whom they pierced.

The spear with which Hitler was obsessed had been discovered at Antioch in 1098 during the First Crusade. It seems that this same lance had been carried as a talisman in the 9th century by Charlemagne, and it was reputed to have helped him win 47 campaigns. It was also said that when Charlemagne accidentally dropped the lance one day, he suddenly fell down dead. The lance then passed into the hands of Heinrich the Fowler, the founder of the royal house of the Saxons, who drove the Poles eastward. The lance later came into the possession of five Saxon monarchs, and generations later, it became the coveted property of the succeeding Hohen-Stauffens of Swabia. The most prominent of this line, Frederick Barbarossa, conquered Italy and even subdued the Pope, forcing him into exile. Barbarossa made the same fatal mistake as Charlemagne; he dropped the lance while wading in a stream in Sicily on his way to the Third Crusade, and within minutes he was dead.

All these stories of the magical lance fired the imagination of the poverty-stricken Austrian. According to Dr Walter Johannes Stein – a prominent mathematician, economist and occultist who had known Hitler in his youth – the future leader of Nazi Germany had a vast understanding of black magic and saw the lance as the equivalent of a magician's wand. In the summer of 1911, Stein visited an occult bookseller in Vienna and bought a worn edition of *Parsival*, an Arthurian romance about the Holy Grail by the 13th century German poet, Wolfram von Eschenbach. The margin of this book was crammed with scribbled notes by someone who evidently had a deep knowledge of the occult – and also a pathological hatred of the Jews. Stein wondered about the book's previous owner, and when he looked at the inside of the flyleaf he found his name: Adolf Hitler.

Stein traced him through the bookseller and spent many hours listening to Adolf's strange views on eugenics and politics, which he found repugnant yet somehow alluring. Stein later said that even though Hitler was only in his early twenties, he felt he had some grand, mystical destiny to fulfil, and radiated a peculiarly evil charisma. One day, the conversation between Stein and Hitler turned to the Holy Lance, and Hitler expressed his belief that the ancient weapon would one day come into his hands, telling Stein of a stirring vision he had witnessed while looking at the lance in its case:

"I slowly became aware of a mighty presence around it, the same awesome presence which I had experienced inwardly on those rare occasions in my life when I had sensed that a great destiny awaited me. A window in the future was opened up to me, through which I saw in a single, illuminating flash, a future event by which I knew, beyond contradiction, that the blood in my veins would one day become the vessel of the Folk-Spirit of my people."

Hitler never divulged the details of his vision, but Stein was convinced that he had probably seen himself 25 years on, in the Heldenplatz outside the Hofburg Museum, addressing thousands of his fellow Austrians. At that very place, on 14 March 1938, the Führer announced his annexation of Austria and ordered the removal of the Hapsburg regalia to the spiritual home of the Nazi movement – Nuremberg. Many historians were baffled by this, as Hitler had always condemned the house of Hapsburg as betrayers of the German race, but they overlooked the legendary reputation of the Spear of Destiny. On 13 October the spear was carefully loaded onto an armoured train with an SS guard and taken over the German border. The relic was then given a new home in the hall of St Catherine's Church, which had been converted into a Nazi war museum. With the lance now in his possession, Hitler seemed drunk with power, yet had a morbid fear of losing the relic, for he knew that those in the past who had let the lance fall from their grasp had soon perished.

Many students of 20th century history have remarked on Hitler's amazing rise to power from his days as a down-and-out postcard painter. It seems that no two historians can agree on whether Hitler was simply in the right place at the right time, or whether he was merely the puppet of some sinister evil genius who lurked in the shadows of the Nazi Party. How Hitler was able, unchecked, for over ten years, to implement policies of unprecedented atrocity, is another question that will continue to plague mankind. Stein believed Hitler's rise to power and his ability to get away with genocide, was due to the dictator's involvement with the black arts. But are there any facts to support Stein's claims?

The official insignia of the Nazi Party was the swastika, a very old symbol that has been found in many cultures across the world, including those of the American Indians and the ancient Greeks. It was usually a symbol representing the sun or good luck, but the Nazi swastika reversed this trend – to denote evil and paganism. The transposed swastika had first been used as an emblem of a neo-pagan movement by the German occultist, Guido von List, in the late 19th century. List renounced his Catholicism at the age of 14 in 1862 and swore he would one day build a grand temple dedicated to Odin, the Scandinavian god of war. Eight years later, List had attracted a sizeable group of like-minded people who also felt a strong spiritual connection with the old mythological deities of Scandinavia. These followers observed the pagan feasts at the solstices and equinoxes, and worshipped the sun as Baldur, the old Norse god who was slain in battle, but rose from the dead – just as the sun rises to end the funereal night. Their sun-worshipping rite was held on the top of a hill in Vienna, and on one occasion, the heathen liturgy ended with List burying eight wine bottles laid out in the shape of his swastika.

When the National Socialist Party was still in its infancy in the 1920s, Hitler realised that the movement needed a symbol. The Russian communists had the hammer and sickle, and Britain had the easily-identifiable Union flag. An interesting suggestion was put forward by a Sternberg dentist named Friedrich Krohn: a black swastika on a white disc, set on a red flag. The red symbolised blood and the social ideal, and the white disc stood for purity of race and nationalism.

The swastika at the centre of all this supposedly signified 'the struggle for victory of the Aryan man'.

Krohn immediately captured Hitler's imagination with his proposal. The most infamous symbol in the history of mankind had been conceived. Shortly after the birth of the Nazi 'cross', Hitler imposed a baffling directive that has never been understood by modern historians; all occult writings and practices were to be rigorously stamped out. Why did someone like Hitler, who was so preoccupied with the occult himself, wish to eradicate occultism?

In 1934, the Berlin police impounded thousands of books on mysticism and the occult. Then came the widespread suppression of all occult groups in Germany – even groups such as the German Order (of which Friedrich Krohn was a member) and the Thule Society – which contained many members of the National Socialist Party, including Rudolf Hess. Hitler's directive to wipe out the occultists seems contradictory, but recent evidence has surfaced which indicates that the Nazi leader attacked the occultists because he saw them as rivals. Similarly, Stalin persecuted and disbanded the occultists in Russia because he feared their secret societies; he also tried to wipe out the ultra-secretive Freemasons. As far as the Führer was concerned, only one occult movement was permissible under his Third Reich – all other competitors would have to be removed.

Among the many accounts we have from people who met the Führer, or worked alongside him, there are recurring stories of his strange powers of persuasion and ability to literally bewitch people. In April 1943, the Italian dictator Mussolini visited Hitler in Germany in a state of deep depression and mental and physical exhaustion. An entry in the diary of Josef Goebbels describes how Hitler revitalised Mussolini:

By putting every ounce of nervous energy into the effort, the Führer succeeded in pushing Mussolini back onto the rails. In those four days, Mussolini underwent a complete change. When he got out of the train on his arrival, the Führer thought he looked like a broken old man. When he left again he was in high fettle, ready for anything.

Hitler's powers of suggestion and motivation were also experienced by Karl Donitz, commander of the U-Boat fleet. Donitz once said of the Führer's uncanny influence:

"I purposely went very seldom to his headquarters, for I had the feeling that I would best preserve my power of initiative and also because, after several days at headquarters, I always had the feeling that I had to disengage myself from his powers of suggestion. I was doubtless more fortunate than his staff, who were constantly exposed to his power and personality."

On another occasion, Dr Hjalmar Schacht, the Nazi Party's financial wizard, asked Hermann Goering to discuss a minor point of economic policy with Hitler. Goering promised he would raise the matter but when he came face to face with Hitler, he found that he could not bring himself to speak. Goering later admitted to Schacht: "I often make up my mind to say something to him, but when I meet him face to face my heart sinks."

Many in the higher echelons of the Nazi Party, as well as SS guards, were convinced that Hitler was possessed. Herman Rauschning, the Governor of Danzig and confidant of the German dictator, claimed that Hitler often suffered terrible nightmares, and awoke many times to see a phantom-like being in his room. Rauschning gives an account of the Führer's night-terror in his book *Hitler Speaks*:

A person close to Hitler told me that he wakes up in the night, screaming and in convulsions. He calls for help, and appears to be half paralysed. He is seized with a panic that makes him tremble until the bed shakes. He utters confused and unintelligible sounds, gasping, as if on the point of suffocation. The same person described to me one of these fits, with details I would refuse to believe had I not complete confidence in my informant.

Hitler was standing up in his room, swaying and looking all round as if he were lost. "It's he, it's he," he groaned; "he's come for me!" His lips were white; he was sweating profusely ... suddenly he screamed: "There! There! Over in the corner!"

But there was nobody in the corner. All the same, Hitler lived in fear of his nocturnal demon. In the Bible several people possessed by demons are described as falling to the floor and frothing at the mouth – during his screaming rages Hitler did the same. Rauschning believed that the man who caused the deaths of more than 30 million people was but a mouthpiece for some evil force:

One cannot help thinking of him as a medium. For most of the time mediums are ordinary, insignificant people. Suddenly they are endowed with what seem to be supernatural powers which set them apart from the rest of humanity. These powers are something that is outside their true personality – visitors, as it were, from another planet. The medium is possessed. Once the crisis is past, they fall back again into mediocrity. It was in this way, no doubt, that Hitler was possessed by forces outside himself – almost demonic forces of which the individual named Hitler was only the temporary vehicle.

Curiously enough, many other observers of Hitler's oratorial skills independently reached the same conclusions as Rauschning. "I looked into his eyes – the eyes of a medium in a trance. Sometimes the speaker's body seemed inhabited by something," Bouchez once remarked.

'The Devil's children have the Devil's luck' is an old adage that certainly applied to Hitler. In World War One, Corporal Hitler fell asleep in a trench and dreamt that a shell killed him. He awoke in a sweat and fled from the spot. The bemused soldier who took his place was blown to bits by an enemy shell minutes later. Then, in 1923, Hitler led a column of National Socialists through the streets of Munich. The police machine-gunned the column, killing 16 storm troopers. Hermann Goering was badly wounded, but Hitler somehow escaped injury. On another occasion, in 1931, Hitler stepped off a pavement in Munich and into the path of a speeding Fiat motorcar, driven by the multi-millionaire, Lord Howard de Walden. Hitler survived the collision without even a bruise, and even shook hands with the speechless de Walden and forgave him. On 20 July 1944, a bomb planted by Colonel Berthold von Stauffenberg under Hitler's conference table exploded. The Führer survived the assassination attempt and Stauffenberg was shot on the following day. His 150 fellow conspirators were also executed.

But Hitler's luck was dealt a severe blow when he allowed the Spear of Destiny to leave him. Because of heavy Allied bombing on Nuremberg in October 1944, Hitler had the spear and the rest of the Hapsburg regalia transferred to a specially constructed reinforced vault.

Within six months, the momentous D-Day landings had been a great success, and the Allies were closing in on the Führer in his Berlin bunker. He knew all hope of victory had long gone, and that it would only be a matter of time before the end came. But for some reason, Hitler waited until 30 April 1945 before he shot himself through the head. It may have been a coincidence, but an ancient occult feast called Walpurgis Night also falls on that day, when hell's demons are said to hold high revelry under their chief – the Devil.

On the day of Hitler's death, Lieutenant William Horn of the American Seventh Army located the Spear of Destiny in its underground bunker. Longinius's famous lance was lying on a bed of red velvet and Horn took possession of the relic on behalf of the United States Government.

EMANUEL SWEDENBORG
The Mystic Who Lived in Two Worlds

No book about mysterious personages would be complete without a description of the psychic scientist, Emanuel Swedenborg, who was born in Stockholm in 1688, the son of Jesper Svedberg, later Bishop of Skara. From an early age, Swedenborg exhibited a remarkable intellect, and in due course he entered Uppsala University. After graduation, Swedenborg travelled widely across Europe to study with the great philosophers and scientists of the day, and, despite a stutter, he mastered most of the European languages during his travels.

Swedenborg excelled at whatever he turned his mind to. As well as being an accomplished musician, he was also highly skilled in mathematics, chemistry, astronomy, anatomy, physics and psychology, and he even anticipated Freudian psychiatry by experimenting with dream analysis. The Swedish savant was also something of an inventor. Although many of his projects were never put into practice, Swedenborg usually sketched the schematics of his creations and worked out the details. Among his inventions were designs for a ship that could become watertight and transform itself into a deadly, armed submarine, a mechanical device which enabled the musical novice to play complicated melodies on almost any instrument, and a hydraulic contraption for the effortless transference of heavy cargo into the hold of a ship.

In 1716, Swedenborg was appointed as the Assessor to the Royal College of Mines, a post he held for 30 years, during which time he vastly improved upon the orthodox methods for extracting metals from rock. In 1718, he published the first book on algebra in Swedish, and it was but the first of a torrent of 40 academic volumes to flow from his quill.

He was ennobled in 1719 and became a member of the Swedish Parliament. But at the height of his accomplishments, many years later when he was in his fifties, Swedenborg discovered that he had other gifts beyond the merely academic. In a letter to a friend, Swedenborg wrote of a life-changing paranormal incident which he had recently experienced:

I have been called to a holy office by the Lord Himself, who most mercifully appeared before me in the year 1743; when he opened my sight into the spiritual world, and enabled me to converse with spirits and angels, in which state I have continued up to the present day. From that time I began to print and publish the various secrets that were seen by me, or revealed to me about heaven and hell, the state of man after death, and the true worship of God.

Swedenborg later gave more details about the incident which proved to be a spiritual milestone in his life. He said he had been in bed when he heard a frightening noise which sounded like 'many winds' rushing through the room. He trembled from head to foot, then something invisible seized him and flung him out of the bed onto the floor. As he clasped his hands to pray for God to deliver him from this unearthly attacker, he felt a hand press against his own, then he beheld the materialisation of a person who resembled Jesus as he is depicted in religious paintings. According to Swedenborg, Jesus told him he had been enlisted into the service of God and would be allowed to talk with angels and the other entities of the spiritual world. However, the exact words spoken by Christ were never fully divulged by Swedenborg. Swedenborg's personality and lifestyle subsequently underwent a dramatic change. He resigned his assessorship, gave up his mundane studies, and devoted the entirety of his time to spiritual development.

About a year after the psychic revelation, Swedenborg was enjoying his usual over-indulgent midday meal, when the room suddenly darkened. Swedenborg looked down at the floor and saw that it was crawling with snakes and toads. A figure then appeared in the corner of the room and told the startled Swede: "Eat not so much!" The darkness and the apparitions faded away and, understandably, Swedenborg decided that it would be wise to eat in moderation from that day on.

Swedenborg gradually developed a variety of psychic talents which included automatic writing, prophecy and precognition. One day he suddenly 'knew' that a friend named Olofsohn would die at precisely 4.45pm. Sure enough, at that exact time, his friend – who was apparently in good health – literally dropped dead. On another occasion, Swedenborg urged a mill owner with whom he was having dinner, to go at once to his mill because a fire was breaking out there. The mill owner knew of his friend's clairvoyant powers and rushed to the mill immediately, where he found a large piece of cloth, which had fallen onto the furnace, ablaze. This peculiar extra-sensory gift is known to students of parapsychology as 'remote viewing', and has been demonstrated in modern times by such psychics as the New York artist, Ingo Swann.

For the remainder of his life, Swedenborg could perceive events far beyond his range of optical vision, but sometimes this uncanny ability was more of a niggling annoyance than a cherished skill. On the Saturday evening of 19 July 1759, Swedenborg was one of 16 guests invited to the home of his friend William Castell in Gothenburg, which is 240 miles from Stockholm. Swedenborg was enjoying dinner with the other guests when he suddenly beheld a stark vision of a massive blaze raging in Stockholm. He told the bemused guests around the table about the fiery vision and became pallid and greatly agitated. He left the house for a breath of fresh air and returned with more details which disturbed a number of the guests. He told one person present that his house had been totally destroyed by the fire and that his own house was now threatened by the hungry flames. He described vividly the course and extent of the raging fire, then suddenly at 8pm, he slumped into a chair out of breath and sighed: "Thank God. The fire is extinguished, the third door from my house."

Many of the guests were still sceptical, but on Monday evening, a messenger arrived from Stockholm and confirmed every detail of Swedenborg's account of the blaze. He had even been right about the way the fire had petered out three doors from his home. When the provisional Governor of Stockholm heard of the strange story, he asked Swedenborg if he knew how the fire had started, and Swedenborg obliged by giving him a blow-by-blow account of the fire's origin.

Swedenborg's alleged ability to converse with spirits is also well-documented. In 1760, the Dutch Ambassador to Stockholm died, and his widow received a bill from a goldsmith who claimed that her deceased husband had not paid for a silver service he had supplied. The widow was distressed at the allegation, for she knew that her husband had been a man who always settled his debts, so she enlisted the services of Swedenborg. The widow asked him if he could get in touch with her dead husband to see if he had indeed paid for the silver service. Swedenborg duly chatted to the ambassador's spirit and was told that he had paid for the silverware, and that the receipt was somewhere in the house. The spirit ended the conversation by promising to return to the house to look for the receipt. Eight days later, the widow had a vivid dream about her departed husband in which he showed her the location of the receipt behind a drawer. When the widow awoke, she anxiously inspected the desk of her late husband, and found the receipt exactly where the dream had indicated.

Another demonstration of Swedenborg's psychic prowess took place in October 1761, when he was summoned by the Queen of Sweden. The Queen inquired if the mystic could get in touch with her brother, Augustus William of Prussia, who had died four years previously. Swedenborg said he would try, and three weeks later returned to the royal court. The Queen was playing cards at the time, and without standing to meet the seer, asked him what information he had. But Swedenborg said her dead brother had asked him to deliver the message – which was highly confidential – to his sister in private. The Queen rose from the card table and gestured to Swedenborg to whisper the message in her ear. Swedenborg reluctantly did so, and whatever it was that he murmured, it caused the Queen to turn pale and totter about as if she was about to faint. When a guard and Swedenborg steadied the monarch, she took a deep breath and trembled as she exclaimed, "That is something which no one else could have told, except my brother!"

In 1772, the founder of Methodism, John Wesley, who had heard so much about the mystical Swede, felt the urge to contact him, but before he did so, imagine his surprise when he received a letter from Swedenborg. It stated:

> *Sir,*
> *I have been informed in the world of spirits that you have a strong desire to converse with me. I shall be happy to see you if you will favour me with a visit. I am, Sir, your humble servant,*
> *Emanuel Swedenborg.*

Wesley was naturally astonished. He wrote back saying that he was delighted at the invitation but could not go immediately, as he was due to embark on a preaching tour soon that would last for six weeks. Swedenborg replied with a letter that shook Wesley even more than the first. In the missive, Swedenborg stated that as he himself would be entering the world of spirits on 29 March, he and Wesley would never meet in this material world.

On 29 March 1772, Emanuel Swedenborg peacefully passed away while in London, and was buried in the Swedish Church of St George of the East. In 1908, his body was reinterred at Stockholm at the request of the Swedish Government. Although Swedenborg made no attempts to preach, or to establish a sect, and never considered himself to be a mystic or a medium, he quickly gained many followers after his death. A distinct denomination was formed in 1787 by several Wesleyan preachers, and the followers called themselves 'the New Church signified by the New Jerusalem in the Revelation'.

Swedenborg's own cosmological beliefs about the 'hereafter' are still being discussed and reinterpreted, but he made it clear in his books and conversations that he believed heaven and hell are all around us, and that death is simply a process by which the soul is transformed to another state. He claimed that the newly arrived spirit in the next world is received by angels and benevolent spirits, and that the novice spirit usually gravitates towards the spirits that are like itself. He courted controversy and risked retribution from the church when he also declared that God punishes no one, but instead transfigures evil spirits by preventing them from indulging in the evil they crave for; he claimed that this was the only type of torture that went on in the next world. Swedenborg also asserted that relatives of the human race lived in countless other worlds in space, and that the spirits of these people from other planets were also in the next world. This far-sighted view predictably caused many in the 18th century to scoff at him, including the German philosopher Kant.

So much for Swedenborg's beliefs; but what have historians and theologians got to say about Swedenborg the man? Like many other extraordinary luminaries, Swedenborg has been branded as a charlatan and a crackpot. He has also been nervously dismissed as a paranoid schizophrenic and even a sexually frustrated swindler. Much has been made of the fact that Swedenborg was jilted in his youth and chose to remain single, although he was attracted to women, but how can this irrelevant trifle detract one iota from Swedenborg's psychic feats and his philosophy? As for the allegations that he was a charlatan, he was always willing to be called on – free of charge – to communicate with spirits, and all his contemporaries described him as sensible, sane, kind, honest and unimpeachable. If we are all headed for an afterlife, perhaps we may get to know more one day about the man who lived in two worlds.

THE ATLANTEANS
Did the Legendary Island of Atlantis Really Exist?

The primary source for the legendary ancient super-civilisation that existed on a mid-Atlantic island, 10,000 years before the birth of Christ, originated in Plato's books *Critias* and *Timaeus*, written around 355 BC, when Plato was in his seventies. In these works, Plato gives a detailed description of the Atlantean metropolis. When describing the dimensions and measurements of the island and its architecture, Plato often refers to the 'stade' – an archaic measurement of length, equivalent to 606 feet 3 inches. According to Plato:

At the centre of the island, near the sea, was a plain, said to be the most beautiful and fertile of all plains, and near the middle of the plain, about 50 stades inland a hill of no great size ... There were two rings of land and three of sea, like cartwheels, with the island at their centre and equidistant from each other ... In the centre was a shrine sacred to Poseidon and Cleito, surrounded by a golden wall through which entry was forbidden ... There was a temple to Poseidon himself, a stade in length, three hundred feet wide and proportionate in height, though somewhat outlandish in appearance. The outside of it was covered all over with silver, except for the figures on the pediment which were covered in gold ... Round the temple were statues of the original ten kings and their wives, and many others dedicated by kings and private persons belonging to the city and its dominions ...

The two springs, cold and hot, provided an unlimited supply of water for appropriate purposes, remarkable for its agreeable quality and excellence; and this they made available by surrounding it with suitable buildings and plantations, leading some of it into basins in the open air and some of it into covered hot baths for winter use. Here separate accommodation was provided for royalty and commoners, and again, for women, for horses and for other beasts of burden ... The outflow they led into the grove at Poseidon, which (because of the goodness of the soil) was full of trees of marvellous beauty and height, and also channelled it to the outer ring-islands by aqueducts at the bridges.

On each of these ring-islands they had built many temples for different gods, and many gardens and areas for exercise, some for men and some for horses ... Finally, there were dockyards full of triremes [ancient galleys] *and their equipment, all in good shape ... Beyond the three outer harbours there was a wall, beginning at the sea and running right round in a circle, at a uniform distance of 50 stades from the largest ring and harbour, and returning in on itself at the mouth of the canal to the sea. The wall was densely built up all round with houses, and the canal and the large harbour were crowded with vast numbers of merchant ships from all quarters, from which rose a constant din of shouting and noise day and night.*

Where was this civilisation sited? According to Plato, Atlantis was located 'Beyond the Pillars of Hercules', which means beyond the Straits of Gibraltar (on either side of which the Herculean pillars once stood) and out into the Atlantic Ocean. Many think that Atlantis was merely a figment of Plato's imagination – a pure myth that the Greek philosopher used as a vehicle for his theories of a Utopia.

Aristotle flatly rejected Plato's tale, and right up to the Middle Ages, most academics agreed with him, even though Aristotlean reasoning on many things, such as metaphysics and astronomy, was faulty, and held up the advancement of empirical science for centuries.

Where did Plato get his information about Atlantis from? He says he heard it from a young man named Critias, who in turn says he heard it from his grandfather, who heard it from his father, a friend of Solon, a famous Greek elder statesman, who had learned of the story from the Egyptian priests of Sais. Solon was visiting Sais on the Nile delta around 600 BC. His job of framing a constitution for Athens and of instituting social and economic reforms had ended, so Solon had decided to devote the remaining years of his life to poetry and the study of history.

He was particularly interested in the origins of the Hellenic civilisation, so he asked the Egyptian scholars what they knew of his nation's genesis.

The scholars of the college of the goddess Neith, the protectress of learning, confided to Solon that there were records in their archives that were thousands of years old which referred to a continent beyond the Pillars of Hercules, which sank around 9,560 BC. This continent was named Atlantis. The people of this continent, the Atlanteans, prized fellowship and friendship above worldly possessions, and enjoyed an advanced system of socialism that meant no one ever lived in poverty. Like the Incas (who were said to be descendants of the Atlanteans) the people of Atlantis also had a moneyless economy and all land was held in common.

Virgil's *Georgics* and Tibullus's *Elegies* state that land in ancient times was shared by large communistic-like societies, where no one had the right to own a single acre. There is also a mention of a lost social system in which 'there were no liars, no sickness, nor old age', in the 5000-year-old Engidu and the poem of Uttra of Sumer.

Alas, this ideal society did not last and Plato says that the Atlanteans eventually became decadent and bellicose. They waged a war against the neighbouring areas of Europe and Asia and not long afterwards Atlantis disappeared beneath the ocean after being devastated by either a catastrophic earthquake, or a meteor. Some sceptical historians believe the dramatic end of Atlantis is a very convenient epilogue that gets around the problem of obtaining proof of the continent's existence.

However, throughout history there have been many instances of land masses sinking and emerging from the sea. In 1780, Falcon Island in the Pacific was discovered by the Spanish, and in 1892 the Government of Tonga planted 2000 coconut palms on the island. Two years afterwards, the island dramatically sank beneath the ocean waves. in November 1963, the volcanic island of Surtsey emerged from the coastal waters of Iceland and grew rapidly. After three weeks, the island – which was half a mile across – had risen to 390 feet above sea level. The lava rapidly solidified and today, the island now has vegetation. in 1819, the delta of the Indus was shaken by a mighty earthquake which caused most of the local territory to sink, but perhaps the worst case of a drowned city occurred on 1 November 1755, when a tremendous earthquake struck Lisbon. Every dwelling in the lower part of the city was demolished by the quake, and a gigantic tidal wave then swept in from the ocean. Over 60,000 people perished in the catastrophe. The shock from the quake was felt over an area of one and a half million miles, and people all over Europe who were attending masses in their cathedrals on that All Soul's Day, actually saw the chandeliers dance and sway.

If Atlantis did disappear under the waves, surely there must be some traces of the island on the bed of the Atlantic? Deep-sea soundings of the Atlantic sea-bed have been made over the years with sonar and submarine investigation, and there have been some very curious finds. In 1898, 500 miles north of the Azores, an American telegraph company lowered grappling irons onto the seabed and tried to retrieve the broken ends of the snapped trans-Atlantic cable. Instead, they brought up samples of basaltic lava. A French geologist named Pierre Termier, who analysed the lava, was flummoxed. He found that the sample was vitreous instead of crystalline, which meant that the lava had been submerged underwater after cooling. As lava disintegrates after 15,000 years, this told Termier that there had been some volcanic activity above sea level near the Azores in the fairly recent past, perhaps around the time of the Atlantis cataclysm.

In other areas of the seabed in the vicinity of the Azores, beach sand has been found. It was first discovered by Professor M Ewing of Columbia University in 1949, at a depth of three and a half miles. The find was just as perplexing as the lava discovery. Beach sand is a product of sea erosion, and usually non-existent on the bed of the ocean, so its presence indicates that coastal land must have sunk into the Atlantic at some period in the past.

Some think that these underwater findings suggest that the Azores are the vestiges of Atlantis, but there is another site in the Atlantic where the legendary continent may have been located: the West Indies. The West Indies consists of an archipelago which extends in a curved chain for over 1,500 miles from the peninsula of Florida to the Venezuelan coast. The islands are mostly volcanic in origin, but the Bahamas and Antigua are composed largely of coral.

In September 1968, a local Bahamian fishing guide, known as 'Bonefish' Sam, brought Dr J Manson Valentine, an archaeologist and honorary curator of the Museum of Science in Miami, to see an intriguing geometrical structure lying in 23 feet of water off North Bimini. Dr Valentine, who had been searching for traces of lost civilisations in the Bahamas for 15 years, was naturally excited.

After investigating the underwater structure, Dr Valentine described his findings in his museum magazine as:

... an extensive pavement of regular and polygonal flat stones, obviously shaped and accurately aligned to form a convincingly artefactual pattern. These stones had evidently lain submerged over a long period of time, for the edges of the biggest ones had become rounded off, giving the blocks the domed appearance of giant loaves of bread or pillows of stone ... Some were absolutely rectangular and some approaching perfect squares.

The J-shaped 'Bimini Road' as it is now called, quickly fired speculation that evidence of a submerged civilisation had been uncovered, perhaps even the very site of Atlantis. Strangely enough, the renowned American psychic and prophet Edgar Cayce (1877-1945) went into a trance in 1933 and said that parts of Atlantis would be discovered in the late 1960s. His actual words were: "A portion of the temples may yet be discovered under the slime of ages and seawater near Bimini. Expect it in '68 or '69 – not so far away." The stones of the Bimini Road cannot be dated, but analysis of the fossilised mangrove roots growing over the stones in the road has dated them at between ten and twelve thousand years old.

In 1975, the explorer Dr David Zink discovered an unusual fragment of worked stone lodged in the Bimini Road: a block of tongue-and-groove masonry. One edge of the man-made fragment is semi-cylindrical and the other rectangular. The remnant is hard but was evidently never fired, which means it cannot be dated by thermo-luminescence, and no archaeologist or architect can identify its origin.

Three miles south of the Bimini Road, underwater explorers have found fluted marble columns, which are hard to explain, as marble is not native to the Bahamas. Around the time of Dr Zink's discovery, Maurice Chatelain, a French space engineer who worked with NASA on the Apollo missions, said he had found a strange reference to the sinking of a continent in an ancient Tibetan scripture. The reference stated that in 9,564 BC a very large part of a continent sank into the ocean in what is now the Caribbean and the Gulf of Mexico. Chatelain believes that the writers of the Tibetan script were themselves Atlanteans who had escaped the disaster.

Beneath the waters of the Great Bahama Banks, a large pyramidal building measuring 180 by 140 feet has been located. In the same area, a pilot spotted a wall under 12 fathoms of unusually clear water. Curiously, the wall had an archway going through the middle of it. There has also been a report recently of another architectural anomaly a few miles from this wall: a large marble citadel covering five undersea acres with roads leading from it. Unfortunately, diving on the citadel is too hazardous, as Cuban patrol boats regularly visit the waters around it.

Surely, if Atlantis did exist in the vicinity of the West Indies, its culture would have rubbed off on the peoples of the eastern coast of Mexico and the North and South Americas? The Aztec capital of Tenochtitlan, which was inhabited by 300,000 people, was situated on an island in a vast lake in the middle of concentric canals. The Aztecs built the capital as a replica of 'Aztlan' – a land which lay in the east, and from which the Aztecs claimed their descent. Tenochtitlan's concentric layout was a copy of the description of Atlantis given by Plato.

The Mayan people of Central America also left curious accounts of the destruction of an early civilisation. Brasseur de Bourbourg, an eminent French ethnographer, deciphered a Mayan document in 1869 which told of the annihilation, many millennia before, of two countries on an island that were rocked by a massive earthquake and 'suddenly disappeared in the night', along with 64 million people.

The American Indians also have stories about a drowned civilisation in their folklore. According to anthropologists, the Indians came across the Bering Straits from Siberia, but the Indians themselves believe that they came from a homeland in the east which was destroyed in a flood. The Okanogan Indians of British Columbia tell a similar story. They maintain that a continent existed in the middle of the Atlantic long ago called 'Samah-tumi-whoo-lah' – which translates as 'White man's island'. This island, which was destroyed in a terrible war, was said to be ruled by a tall, white-skinned ruler named Queen Scomalt.

In the year 1519, Hernan Cortes and his conquistadors landed in Mexico at Vera Cruz. Cortes and his men gazed in awe at Mexico City, the capital of the New World. The Emperor Montezuma II greeted the explorers and promptly surrendered himself and his empire of five million people to Cortes and his 600 soldiers. Cortes was baffled. He was not aware that to the Aztecs and Mayas, his arrival signified the Second Coming. Like the Red Indians of North America, the races of Central America were awaiting the return of the White God, known as Quetzacoatl or Viracocha to the Incas, who was expected to turn up soon. The Toltecs described the god as fair and ruddy with a beard and long hair, wearing a long robe of black linen cut low at the neck with short sleeves – a form of dress worn by the natives to this very day.

To the baffled Cortes, the Emperor explained (through the daughter of an Aztec chieftain, who acted as an interpreter) that the Aztecs had not lived in Mexico long, and that their ancestors had been led by a bearded white man from the east named Quetzacoatl, who displayed great wisdom. Before sailing back towards the east, the White God had promised to return to Mexico to govern the land. Cortes could make no sense of the Emperor's story, and gave an account of his journey from Cuba and his mission to secure the pagan lands for King Charles V of Spain. The Emperor replied:

"You tell us that you come from where the sun rises, the things you tell us of this great lord or king who sent you hither to us, we believe and take it for certain that he is our natural lord, especially as you tell us that he has known of us for many days. And therefore you may be certain that we shall obey you and accept you as lord in place of this great lord of whom you speak."

Unfortunately, the Emperor could not dissuade Cortes and his gold-crazed conquistadors from proceeding to Tenochtitlan. He was held hostage, but won the affection of his captors. However, the white visitors caused an uprising among the natives, and as Montezuma tried to address them, they showered him with stones, and he died several days later.

Fourteen years later, the same tragedy unfolded in Peru, where Atahualpa, the tyrannical Inca ruler, venerated the Spanish soldier of fortune, Don Francisco Pizarro, as a descendant of the White God Viracocha. In shining armour, Pizarro and 168 soldiers had been sighted by the natives, riding inland from the sea towards the Inca city of Cajamarca. The awestruck Incas greeted the strange visitors, and at Cajamarca, Atahualpa hailed Pizarro as the divine son of Viracocha. When Pizarro gave a demonstration of his power by firing a cannon, the Incas shuddered, as they recalled the legends which told of Viracocha's control over thunder. In no time, Pizarro's men were plundering their way across the country.

Atahualpa saw that the visitors were not gods, but gangsters, and he demanded that the thieves from the West return the goods they had stolen. Instead, Pizarro sent a Bible-carrying priest to convert the Inca ruler and his people from sun-worship to Christianity, but the catechism lesson ended abruptly when Atahualpa threw the holy book to the ground. The outraged Spaniards immediately went on the rampage and slaughtered the unarmed natives. Atahualpa was taken captive and held for ransom for nine months, and during this time, a huge room was filled with silver and gold and offered to Pizarro for the Inca ruler's release. But Pizarro had already planned to kill Atahualpa in order to disrupt and conquer the Inca society, and after arranging a mock trial, he found Atahualpa guilty of trumped-up charges.

Pizarro gave him a choice: he could be burned alive as a heathen, or he could be strangled as a Christian. Atahualpa chose to be strangled. He was baptised Juan de Atahualpa 'in honour of St John the Baptist' then tied to a stake and garrotted. Pizarro and his soldiers then laid on a full-scale Catholic funeral for the 'converted' ruler. It was then only a matter of time before the 'men from the rising sun' sacked the rest of the country.

The strange aspect of these dark episodes in the exploration of the Americas is the way in which the explorers were assumed to be long-awaited white gods from an eastern land. If Atlantis really was situated near the West Indies, there is evidence that an earthquake may not have been the cause of the demise of the legendary land mass. On the ocean floor of the south-west Atlantic, near Puerto Rico, there are twin depressions 23,000 feet deep, which look remarkably like craters. There are similar craters of meteoric origin on the North American mainland at Arizona and Charleston, South Carolina, where an elliptical area extends out into the Atlantic. It has been estimated that the craters near the hypothetical site of Atlantis in the West Indies, were created with an explosive force equivalent to the detonation of 30,000 million tonnes of nitro-glycerine, between 10 and 15,1000 BC. An explosion of this magnitude could also be produced by 3000 medium-sized hydrogen bombs. Such an apocalyptic explosion would punch a hole in the planet's crust and some theorists think that this was how the Gulf of Mexico was formed millions of years before.

The celestial object that inflicted such a devastating hammer blow to the Earth is estimated to have been around six miles in diameter, which rates it as an asteroid. An earlier asteroid fall is thought to have wiped out the dinosaurs 65 million years ago, and in modern times, our world has had a number of close shaves with so-called 'Earth-grazers' – asteroids which come dangerously close to the planet as they orbit the sun. The asteroid Eros, which has a diameter of ten miles, came within 14 million miles of the Earth in 1931. In February 1936, another asteroid named Adonis came within one and a half million miles of the Earth, which is too close for comfort.

Incredibly, in 1993, an asteroid designated 1993 KA2 made the closest approach to our planet ever made by an asteroid. It passed within 90,000 miles of the Earth, travelling at a speed of 48,000 miles per hour. Although it was only 30 feet in diameter, the asteroid had an estimated mass of 6000 tons, and had it survived a fiery plunge through Earth's atmosphere, it would have caused the equivalent of an atomic explosion. Despite all the speculation, the truth about Atlantis still eludes us, yet the legends of the submerged civilisation continue to hold a growing fascination for each generation. There are many who think Atlantis is just a fable, but they should remember that prior to the excavations made by the explorer Heinrich Schliemann in the late 19th century, the city of Troy was also regarded as fiction.

CHARLES WELLS
How Did He Break the Bank at Monte Carlo?

In 1654, the Chevalier de Mere, a French gambler, wrote to Pierre Fermat and Blaise Pascal, two of France's mathematical giants, with a number of problems concerning the nature of his disreputable pastime. Thanks to de Mere, mathematics now has the Theory of Probability, which allows us to discover how likely an event is through the following formula: the number of events that are favourable to our outcome, divided by the total number of all possible events.

For example, let's say the French gambler wanted to throw a dice once and come up with a six; his chances, according to the formula, are one in six, because the number of events favourable to his outcome equals one (he has one throw), and the total number of all possible events is six (the six sides of the dice). Similarly, if the gambler tosses a coin in the air, the probability of it landing on heads is one in two.

But this theory only tells the gambler what odds to expect; it doesn't tell him when the die will come up with a six. Ideally, what the gambler would like is a mathematical method that can reliably predict what the outcome of a particular event will be, but as yet, the world's mathematicians have failed to produce such a theory. The nearest they have come to the gambler's dream is in the extrapolation technique, which is a way of predicting, alas, with a margin of error, the future of a quantity from the past values of that quantity. For example, by extrapolating, we can predict what a country's population figure will be in a hundred years' time, by studying that country's past rate of population increase.

Sadly, extrapolation is useless when no past data is known, so it seems that the gamblers' search for the perfect system is but a dream. Or is it? Perhaps not, for it is a mathematical fact that even with random events there are definite clusterings of coincidences. Therefore, if we toss a coin 1,024 times, it is highly likely that there will be one run of eight tails in a row, two of seven in a row, four of six in a row, and eight runs of five in a row. No one is sure why these clusters occur, but several mathematicians believe that there are undiscovered laws which govern such coincidences, and once they are worked out, it will be possible to predict the outcome of the toss of a coin, the throw of a dice, or the spin of the roulette wheel.

In 1891, a mysterious corpulent Englishman calling himself Charles Deville Wells, strolled into Monte Carlo's world-famous casino and placed even money bets on red and black. He proceeded to win almost every time, despite the astronomical odds that were stacked against him. When his winnings surpassed the 100,000 francs limit allocated to the table, the attendants closed the 'bank', covered the table with a black 'mourning' cloth and closed it for the remainder of the day. On his third and final visit to the casino, Wells pulled off an extraordinary feat. He placed his first bet on number five (35 to 1 odds), and his gamble was a success. The attendants were stunned and suspicious. Wells then added his winnings to the original bet and placed the entire amount on number five again. The roulette wheel was spun and after a tense wait it did indeed come up again. This incredible outcome happened five times in succession. Wells collected his mammoth winnings and left the casino as the enraged, but baffled attendants looked on.

Wells bought a yacht and settled in the south of France, but people eager to know his gambling system persecuted him wherever he went. He was finally arrested by French police, charged with fraud, and extradited back to England. He stood trial at the Old Bailey, where he admitted to having 20 aliases, but he never revealed his real name. He was sentenced to an eight-year prison sentence, and after his release moved to Paris, where he died in poverty in 1926.

How did Wells foresee what numbers would come up at the roulette table? Was he using some abstruse mathematical system to predict the outcomes of the wheel? The systems used by gamblers are legion and legendary, but not one of them is infallible. They range from complicated mathematical tables, the result of many years of study, to even more complex, computer-aided hypotheses concerning the chaos and catastrophe theory. The simplest system is said to be the Martingale, which closely resembles the betting practice commonly known as 'double or quits on the toss of the coin'.

Imagine you have won ten dollars from a gambling opponent. You say to him 'Double or quits on the toss of the coin'. If he wins, the ten dollar debt is cancelled, but if you win, his situation is twice as bad as before, and you can continue in this way until the account is squared. The rule for playing a Martingale against the bank at a casino is as follows: You back a colour say, red, consistently and double your stake each time you lose, reverting after a win to your original stake. Therefore, every red shows you a profit of one plaque over and above whatever you may have lost on that series. Compared with other ways of betting, the Martingale system makes you more likely to win than lose, but you will lose greater amounts, and should your run of bad luck come early in the proceedings, you may well find your capital so diminished, that you simply cannot wait for luck to take a more favourable turn.

Charles Wells was closely watched by other gamblers at the roulette table. One of them wrote of the lucky Englishman's system:

Wells began with ten units, decreasing his stake by one if he won, increasing by one if he lost, so that his last stake, if he lost consecutively, was twenty. He stopped playing after winning all ten coups with a gain of 55 units, made up of thus: 10 plus 9 plus 8 plus 7 plus 6 plus 5 plus 4 plus 3 plus 2 plus 1 = 55. The weak point in this system was that, though he won 55 units if a run of ten occurred at once in his favour, he lost 165 units if a run of ten occurred at once against him.

Amazingly, the miracle happened frequently enough for Wells to break the bank. But Mr Wells hinted that he had actually used a far more advanced system than the luck-dependent Martingale. He insinuated that his successful method of winning was in fact an algorithm based on the layout of the roulette board used in Monte Carlo and in most casinos of southern France where he played. The board is numbered from 1 to 36, 18 of the numbers being black and 18 red. But there is a zero, which offsets the odds in favour of the house by 37 to 36 on any single number bet.

Wells implied that numbers could be predicted from past numbers that had come up on the wheel. This seems to be nonsensical, but Wells stared intently at the wheel whenever the ball landed on a number, and appeared to be muttering, perhaps performing mental calculations. According to traditional mathematics, gamblers basing their bets on past outcomes are committing a gross error, because in the world of probability, the past has no influence on the future. If there have been 20 successive reds at the roulette table, it does seem likely that black will turn up, but the laws of probability state that this simply isn't so – red is just as likely to turn up again. However, those who eaves-dropped on Wells at the table claimed that the gambler believed he had discovered some sort of natural recurring series of numbers that turn up everywhere.

The 13th century mathematician, Leonardo Fibonacci, discovered that such sequences occur naturally in nature. His so-called 'Fibonacci Sequence' is: 0,1,1,2,3,5,8,13,21,34, ... etc, each number being the sum of the previous two. The Fibonacci sequence has turned out to be relevant to the natural world in many ways. For instance, botanists have noted that the leaves on a branch are often situated helically around the stalk at measurements that correspond to Fibonacci's sequence. The same sequence is to be found in the proportions and ratios of many other natural patterns, such as the pads of a cat's paw and the spirals of a snail's shell.

Fibonacci's Sequence had been partly discovered in ancient Greece, where architects employed a 'mystical ratio' known as the 'golden section'. This ratio, which is approximately equal to 1.618, occurs over and over again in the proportions of the human body, the spiral galaxies of the universe, the layout of seeds in a sunflower, and in many other diverse locations, but no one knows why 1.618 is so omnipresent.

There are other naturally recurring decimals (for example 0.1428571) but sometimes the significance of these numbers is baffling. Take the Greek letter π (pi) which, as every school child knows, is the ratio of the circumference of any circle to its diameter, and is approximately equal to 3.1415. Thanks to the computer, π has now been calculated to over 200 million decimal places, and deep within the millions of figures which make it up, computers have discovered that there is a bizarre 'cyclically increasing sequence' of digits that start with 89012345 and are gradually turned around to become 2109876543. It is as if there is some design among the never-ending string of numbers, but why the recurrent numbers are there continues to puzzle mathematicians.

So, as we have seen, mathematics is much more than the study of measurements, numbers and quantities. It is a science that is far from complete, and seems to be heading towards the metaphysical. It is a well-known fact that many discoveries in any systemised branch of knowledge come about long before their time. Is it possible that Charles Wells stumbled upon a mathematical discovery relating to the strange phenomenon of recurring numbers that has so far had eluded the mathematicians? Or is the truth more sinister? Until we know more, Wells will be best remembered as the subject of an old Charles Coburn music hall song: *The Man Who Broke the Bank at Monte Carlo.*

OTHER TITLES BY TOM SLEMEN

HAUNTED LIVERPOOL 1	Tom Slemen	£5.99
HAUNTED LIVERPOOL 2	Tom Slemen	£5.99
HAUNTED LIVERPOOL 3	Tom Slemen	£5.99
HAUNTED LIVERPOOL 4	Tom Slemen	£5.99
HAUNTED LIVERPOOL 5	Tom Slemen	£5.99
HAUNTED LIVERPOOL 6	Tom Slemen	£5.99
HAUNTED LIVERPOOL 7	Tom Slemen	£5.99
HAUNTED LIVERPOOL 8	Tom Slemen	£5.99
HAUNTED LIVERPOOL 9	Tom Slemen	£5.99
HAUNTED LIVERPOOL 10	Tom Slemen	£5.99
HAUNTED LIVERPOOL 11	Tom Slemen	£5.99
HAUNTED LIVERPOOL 12	Tom Slemen	£5.99
HAUNTED LIVERPOOL 13	Tom Slemen	£5.99
HAUNTED LIVERPOOL 14	Tom Slemen	£5.99
STRANGE LIVERPOOL	Tom Slemen	£5.99
HAUNTED WIRRAL	Tom Slemen	£5.99
LIVERPOOL GHOST WALK	Tom Slemen	£5.99
HAUNTED CHESHIRE	Tom Slemen	£5.99
WICKED LIVERPOOL	Tom Slemen	£5.99
Mysterious World	Tom Slemen	£5.99
HAUNTED LIVERPOOL ANTHOLOGY	Tom Slemen	£6.99
HAUNTED LIVERPOOL double cassette and audio book read by Tom Slemen		£8.99

Available from all good bookshops

For a free stocklist contact:

THE BLUECOAT PRESS
329 Mariners House, Queens Dock Commercial Centre
Norfolk Street, Liverpool L1 0BG

Telephone: 0151 707 2390
Website: www.bluecoatpress.co.uk